C000129260

AN OLD RADICAL AND HIS BROOD

Engraving of John Bowring 1826 from a painting by B. E. Duppa

AN OLD RADICAL AND HIS BROOD

G. F. Bartle

A portrait of Sir John Bowring and his family,
based mainly on the correspondence of Bowring and his son,
Frederick Bowring

JANUS PUBLISHING COMPANY
London, England

FOR MY WIFE AND FAMILY

First published in Great Britain 1994
by Janus Publishing Company
Edinburgh House, 19 Nassau Street,
London W1N 7RE

Copyright © George F. Bartle 1994

British Library Cataloguing in Publication Data
A catalogue record for this book is available
from the British Library.

ISBN 1 85756 132 5

All rights reserved. No part of this publication
may be reproduced, stored in a retrieval system or
transmitted in any form or by any means, electronic,
mechanical, photocopying, recording or otherwise,
without the prior permission of the publisher.

The right of George F. Bartle to be identified
as the author of this work has been asserted by
him in accordance with the Copyright, Designs
and Patents Act 1988.

Printed and bound in England by
Antony Rowe Ltd, Chippenham, Wiltshire

Contents

The author is grateful to the John Rylands University Library of Manchester for permission to reproduce extracts from the Bowring Papers (English MSS 1228–1232)

Preface

There has been an increase in interest in Sir John Bowring during
the last 35 years. Two conferences, one in London, one in his birth-
place, Exeter, have recently been held and various articles, covering
many aspects of his astonishingly varied career, have appeared in
print. Some previous misconceptions about him have been removed
and much fresh information about his activities has come to light.
The present work does not claim to be a full biography (which
would require resources beyond present means) but provides enough
information about Bowring himself to put his family affairs in their
setting. For these, the main sources are the extensive correspondence
deposited in the John Rylands Library at Manchester nearly 40 years
ago, especially Bowring's correspondence with his sons Frederick
and Edgar and Frederick Bowring's correspondence with his parents.
Most of the other information about Bowring comes from sources
indicated in articles and books already published by various people,
including the present author whose original thesis on Bowring's
political career was accepted by London University in 1959.

After careful consideration it was decided not to burden the
account with a display of footnotes and marginal comments, but a
detailed list of sources is given at the end. The dates of family
letters, however, are indicated in the text. The frequent abbreviations,
especially in Frederick Bowring's letters, (which he explains to his
mother as a 'lawyer's habit'), e.g. 'wd' for 'would', 'cd' for 'could',
have been ironed out and also the abbreviations for 'and'. On the
other hand, Bowring's frequent use of a dash, where a comma or
semi-colon would seem more appropriate, has been retained as it
preserves the character of his letter-writing which, at its best, could
be very expressive.

As this is primarily a study of Bowring's relations with his family, certain episodes in his career, such as his role on the London Greek Committee, his administrative problems as governor of Hong Kong, his dealings with his foreign verse collaborators, are only considered in outline. More information on these and many other matters is available in the works mentioned in the sources. As regards the extent of Bowring's Utilitarian and 'Necessarian' convictions, I leave this question to more erudite scholars on both sides of the Atlantic, merely observing that Bowring himself confessed to Frederick that his mind 'had always been too desultory . . . his knowledge too super-ficial for abstract conceptions.'

Bowring has frequently been described as a 'Victorian' (e.g. in the published papers of the Exeter conference held in 1992). It is there-fore worth noting that much of his career, including his relations with Bentham, his editorship of the *Westminster Review*, the majority of his verse translations and sacred verses, most of his commercial missions, his first years in Parliament and the first two volumes of *Minor Morals*, all belong to the period before Victoria came to the throne. He was, in fact, a figure of the post-Napoleonic era and much of his radicalism and many of his literary productions express the spirit of that romantic and turbulent age. His free trade and liberal reform activities as an MP are, indeed, characteristic of the Victorian period whilst his actions in China contain more than a hint of later Victorian imperialism. The true Victorian is, of course, Frederick Hermann Bowring (probably named after Goethe's romantic hero) with his earnestness, religious preoccupations, literary tastes and self-questioning, not to mention his love of mountains and walking holi-days. One would like to know more about Frederick and his brothers and sisters.

G.F.B.
January 1993

1

The Old Radical when Young

John Bowring was born on 17 October 1792 at Larkbeare (or Great Larkbeare) in the parish of St Leonard's, Exeter, close to the north bank of the river Exe. He was the eldest son of a cloth merchant, Charles Bowring, who, though a Unitarian, had married the daughter of the Anglican clergyman of St Ives, Sarah Anne Lane, on 6 November 1791. (The occasion was important enough to be reported in the *Gentleman's Magazine*.) The family business had been established in the time of Charles II when a certain John Bowring of Chulmleigh sold his estate in north Devon and settled near Exeter. Successive generations of Bowrings had made a comfortable living from the West Country cloth trade, which flourished until the early 19th century when it had to face the competition of the revolutionised cloth industry of the industrial north. In Charles Bowring's day, however, trade was still good and even the Napoleonic Wars had few permanent ill-effects upon it, the Bowrings exporting serges (coarse woollens) to the Iberian Peninsula and latterly to China. Indeed, Bowring's father was able to purchase the freehold of the property at Larkbear (as it was usually spelt at this period) in 1822 from his landlord, Thomas Baring, who resided in the neighbouring Mount Radford estate.

Bowring was one of nine children born between 1792 and 1808, of whom only five survived their first years. With the exception of his elder sister, Margaret, who died at the age of 21, he was the only one of his parents' offspring to marry and raise a family. His sisters Anne and Lucy Jane both remained spinsters (though Anne may have received a proposal from one of Bowring's brothers-in-law) and his brother, Charles, 16 years younger than himself, stayed a bachelor.

Little is known about Bowring as a child. Born in the year France became a republic, he grew up against the background of a series of European wars. There is no independent information about him apart from one piece of gossip about some trivial dishonesty, passed on by Harriet Martineau who had little good to say of most of her male contemporaries and particularly disliked Bowring. The main source for his early years, the *Autobiographical Recollections of Sir John Bowring*, somewhat hastily edited after his death by his son Lewin, draws many of the anecdotes about his boyhood from earlier accounts. Bowring himself must have related many stories about the early Exeter years to his family. Some reminiscences of 'Exeter Sixty years Ago' were written by Bowring for Dickens's journal *All the Year Round*, but they tell us little about his own early days. In his youth Bowring, like his sons, seems to have been studious. According to Lewin, who read some of his father's boyhood letters (which, unlike Frederick Bowring's letters, do not seem to have survived), he displayed 'a strong religious feeling tinged with a didactic and moralizing tone which seems strongly at variance with the natural buoyancy of youth'. *The Autobiographical Recollections* mention a sister who received a tip for waking him early so that he could study. (A similar story about himself is told by Frederick Bowring many years later.) There is no reason to doubt Bowring's claim that his childhood was a happy one. His mild and unambitious father used 'no other discipline than that of kind reproof', while his mother, from whom he inherited his quickness with figures and adeptness at keeping accounts, left her children mainly to servants. An important influence on Bowring's early years was his grandfather, who lived at Little Larkbeare opposite the family residence and survived until Bowring was 13. A man of strong personality and radical opinions, he was a resolute opponent of the slave trade and served in various leading positions at George's Meeting House, the local Unitarian chapel in South Street, then at the height of its prestige amongst the pillars of Exeter non-conformity. (A portrait bust of Bowring stood in the chapel until it was closed.) There is no need to doubt the importance of Unitarianism on Bowring during his formative years nor the close connection of the Bowring family with the chapel. Indeed Bowring's sister, Margaret, was to marry a son of the minister, James Kenrick. Restricted as they were, until 1813, from freedom of worship and, until 1828, by the Test and Corporation Acts, from an active part in public life, the Unitarians formed a closely knit community. In Bowring's words, 'they took to money-making, as persecuted people frequently do, and found compensation . . . in doing better from a worldly point of view than most of their neighbours'.

Such formal education as Bowring received was mainly at a Unitarian institution. After attending 'Mr Bowden's school' in Paris Street, Exeter, he was sent by his pious father to a small Unitarian boarding academy at Moretonhampstead on Dartmoor, where he remained for two years. This school was run, not very efficiently, by the minister, James Bransby who got into trouble with the law for forgery. After leaving this school at which he claims to have received some encouragement for his literary skills but little else (apart from a supply of schoolboy anecdotes which appear in his *Recollections*), Bowring went to work as a clerk at the age of 13, first in his father's business and then in the counting house of the local firm of Kennaway and Co., whose trade in woollen goods and wines with the Iberian Peninsula was one of the largest in the West Country. According to Bowring, Robert Kennaway encouraged his proficiency in languages and Bowring started keeping a journal which he wrote up each day in a different tongue. The foreign traders on the Exeter quayside provided a readily available source of information and he practised Spanish and Italian with itinerant barometer sellers, German and Dutch with a Quaker merchant and picked up French from a refugee priest. He correctly discovered that the best way to learn a language was to speak it and 'get rid of the notion of verbally translating the phrase'.

It was during the years when he was working at Kennaways that Bowring came under the influence of Dr Lant Carpenter, who took over the ministry at George's Meeting on the death of Kenrick in 1805. A man of strong personality, high intelligence and considerable pedagogical skill – he opened his first school when he was at Exeter – Carpenter possessed the moral earnestness of the Unitarian ministers of the age. His coldness with adults melted away in the company of boys and 'the cordiality of his manner would kindle their attachment to himself almost to enthusiasm'. With Bowring, who attended his evening study group, his attitude was somewhat ambiguous, though Bowring undoubtedly learned much from him and later described him as 'one of the best of men' and the most important mentor of his youth.

At the age of 18 Bowring was sent to London as a clerk for

Milford and Co., a prominent Exeter firm with a London branch, then providing supplies of food and material for Wellington's forces in the Peninsula. It was probably because of his increasing fluency in Spanish that Milford sent him in 1813 to the battlefield area near San Sebastian with cargoes of wheat and stores for the army. He seems to have remained in the north of Spain and the Bordeaux area of France until late in 1814. This was Bowring's first journey abroad and he discovered, as he was to do many years later at Canton, a great deal of corruption, everything being 'bought at extravagant prices', the army being 'at the mercy of contractors, jobbers, speculators in exchange and a 1,000 classes of adventurers, English and foreign'. After a short period back in London, Bowring returned to the Peninsula in 1815, visiting Portugal where it was his duty to negotiate for the settlement of outstanding claims on supplies for the army provided by his firm. On his return to England, however, his employment by Milford came to an end. According to Bowring this was because he was not satisfied with Milford's estimate of his services. Perhaps Milford had reprimanded Bowring for failing in his difficult debt-collecting mission to Portugal and Bowring had taken offence.

Whatever the reasons for the dismissal, Bowring was now jobless and after some uncertainty set up as a merchant on his own account. The details of this first venture are obscure, for Bowring speaks of it only in the vaguest terms. He had 'acquired a small property amounting to about £1500'; he attempted to support his enterprise on this but his capital proved too little. He probably tried to take advantage of his knowledge of Spanish to exploit the possibilities which restored British influence in the Peninsula had provided and, as on later occasions, speculated beyond his means. At any rate after this failure he decided to seek a partner and in 1818 established the firm of Bowring and Co. in conjunction with a certain Henry Murdoch at 23 Bucklersbury, Cheapside. Later Bowring and Co. moved to Freeman's Court, Cornhill and then to Jeffrey Square, St Mary Axe (now occupied by the Baltic Exchange). The principal business of the firm was the shipment of herrings to France and the Iberian Peninsula and the importation of wines. For a time there was a subsidiary branch at Gibraltar, named Bowring and Murdoch. Murdoch remains rather a shadowy figure. He reappears in Bowring's correspondence when Bowring was governor of Hong Kong and

4

Murdoch and his wife were living in straitened circumstances. Bowring sent them some money. One of Bowring's business contacts was probably William Alexander of Great Yarmouth, a prominent local Unitarian, with whom Bowring frequently corresponded. Another was the firm of Martineau and Co. of Norwich.

In his early years in London Bowring could not afford the time or money to live in a smart residential suburb, such as Hackney or Highgate, and lodged near Cheapside with a 'pamphlet writer' named Parkes, who encouraged his interest in literature. (Carpenter had been suspicious of works of the imagination.) But he soon established links with Hackney, which was one of the main centres of Unitarianism in the capital, the minister of the New Gravel Pit Congregation, Revd Robert Aspland, being an acquaintance of Lant Carpenter. Bowring began to take a part in New Gravel Pit affairs, assisting in the formation of a Non-Con Club and reading papers advocating civil and religious liberty. He served on the executive committee of the congregation between 1818 and 1825 and was prominent enough for one of its meetings to be held at his counting-house in Jeffrey Square during repairs to the chapel vestry. Local records reveal that there were other Bowrings in the Hackney area, one of whom, Samuel Bowring, was a schoolmaster, but it is not clear what their connections were with the Exeter family. Other prominent Unitarians included William Johnston Fox, minister of the Finsbury chapel, and Bowring's future brother-in-law, George Kenrick, son of the former minister of George's Meeting.

It was probably in Unitarian circles at Hackney that Bowring first became acquainted with the Lewin family and met Maria Lewin, younger daughter of Samuel Lewin, a corn merchant in the City who resided in Mare Street, Hackney. She had two brothers, Samuel Hawtayne and Thomas Fox Lewin and several sisters. Her eldest sister, Anne, was married in 1814 to Thomas Asline Ward, a Sheffield business man and Unitarian and it is from his diaries that we get our earliest information about Maria's contacts with Bowring. We learn that she had an earlier suitor who was not favoured by her family or herself. In 1813, two years after Bowring's arrival in London, Ward, who was courting her sister, noted in his diary the dawnings of another romance, for in the evening 'Mr John Bowering who stayed to supper, brought his flute and practised with Maria'. A year later Ward recorded that Bowring's 'attentions to that lady were

5

becoming more marked'. Bowring and Maria were married at Hackney on 16 September 1816 in the presence of Bowring's father and sister Margaret and members of the Lewin family and they had their honeymoon at Exeter. Maria probably brought Bowring a dowry, which provided the capital enabling him to set up as a merchant on his own account. After the marriage Bowring and his wife took up residence in a smart area of Hackney near London Fields. The census returns for 1821 list the household as consisting of eight people, six of them women, so in addition to Bowring's wife and infant daughter, there were probably several domestic servants. In the mid-1820s other members of the Lewin family were living near London Fields and continued to reside there when Bowring and his family were obliged to leave the area. Comfortably established, Bowring and his wife began to hold dinner parties at one of which the Unitarian minister, Fox, remarked on 'the youthful appearance of our host and hostess. Mrs Bowring has a very young look full of modesty and simplicity. At first you would look about for her mother and elder sister but a second glance discovered something of the manner that indicated the mistress of the house'. With Bowring himself, Fox wrote to his future wife, Eliza, 'you would have been irretrievably in love. Looking divinely, exchanging a bit of French and Italian with ladies who wanted to show off ... conversing in Spanish with a Spanish patriot ... who speaks little or no English and all this and much more without the least appearance of bustle or effect'.

It is difficult to form an impression of Maria Bowring in her youth. Compared with her husband's vast correspondence, much of which has survived, there are only three of her early letters. She was clearly a well-educated woman of energy and resolution, who shared many of the opinions of her husband, to whom she was devoted. Many years later Bowring wrote to his son Frederick from Canton, 'I do not think there is wisdom in delaying marriage too long ... A fit marriage is such a security against the ills and errors of life that I would rather see a too early than a too late engagement. With all my troubles I owe to my marriage every hope and every bliss which are dearest and my children may profit by a father's experience'. It comes as rather a surprise after this to discover some lines of verse in Bowring's writing among the Bentham papers, perhaps written after a quarrel:

> I have got a plaguey wife
> Cold and proud and prudish
> And she harrasses my life
> Makes me rough and rudish.

In December 1818 their first daughter, Maria, was born at Hackney. 'I am too – happy (may I say) to add more', Bowring wrote to his sister-in-law, Anne Ward, at Sheffield. The Bentham papers contain another fragment of verse:

> When I am good, I'm glad and gay
> And then my mother smiles on me
> And then I hear my father say
> Come, come and dance upon my knee
> But when Maria does what's wrong
> Her mother has no smiles to give
> And from her father's silent tongue
> Maria will no praise receive.

In 1819, after the birth of Maria, Bowring again visited the continent in an attempt to extend his business contacts, travelling to Spain, France and the Netherlands. Like many other young men in the post-war years, he had developed radical opinions and was making the acquaintance 'of many well-known liberals'. On his return to England he brought out what was probably his first publication, some 14 pages of *Observations on the State of Religion and Literature in Spain*, containing some verses but mainly consisting of an attack on the Catholic priests and the Inquisition. After a brief period back with his family, Bowring embarked late in 1819 on one of his more ambitious tours, which took him right across northern Europe through Germany to Russia and back through Scandinavia. No letters to his family and friends have survived from this tour and we depend on *Autobiographical Recollections*. At St Petersburg he claims to have attended a court ball where he 'talked in French with the Chief of Police, one of the most distinguished noblemen in Russia' and in Sweden he visited the Bishop of Orebro who wrote 'some pretty lines' in his album. It is difficult to know what to make of Bowring's anecdotes: Louis Philippe symbolically falling off his armchair, Bentham threatening unwelcome visitors with his stick, the short-sighted King of Denmark colliding with Bowring and the Duke of

7

Schleswig-Holstein 'deeply engaged in Phallic rites'. Perhaps they are the reverse side to the flattery and obsequiousness which so many acquaintances allege against Bowring, especially during his youth.

The journey to Russia was the earliest of many long absences from his wife and family which Bowring was to make in the coming years. He was by no means the only Englishman to make long visits to the continent, including Russia, after the Napoleonic wars when foreign tours again became possible. (The Quaker philanthropist, William Allen, comes readily to mind.) It is clear that Bowring's journeys had as much to do with making contacts for foreign verse translations as with trade. On his return from Russia he published the first volume of *Specimens of the Russian Poets* 'by John Bowring FLS', a novelty which received some public acclaim and launched him on his literary career. (Verses from the collection were to be included in school readers for many years.) The revolts against Napoleon had stirred up a consciousness of national identity among little-known peoples and produced an enthusiasm for their folk literature and customs. Russia, indeed, was hardly in this category, as one of the victorious Great Powers, but little had previously been known in England of its literature. Bowring's Russian volume was dedicated to the philologist Friedrich Adelung, who had provided Bowring with translations of Russian verse in German and English, given him information about Russian poets and looked after the sale of Bowring's book on the continent in return for assistance in England with his own publications. This process of mutual cooperation with foreign scholars was followed by Bowring for most of his verse translations from unfamiliar tongues, laying the foundation for his reputation as a 'monster of languages'.

During his long absences from home it has to be asked whether Bowring, a young and gregarious man anxious to make advantageous contacts, remained faithful to his marriage vows. As Bentham was later to remind him, Bowring was 'in no want of enemies' and the correspondence and diaries of the age, not to mention the newspaper and journal reports on his many activities, particularly during his election campaigns, were to accuse him of every degree of obsequiousness, vanity, miscalculation and deceit: 'the busyest of busybodies and the slipperiest', an 'atheist' and 'republican'. But never once in this scurrilous age does there appear any allegation of personal dissoluteness. During his commercial missions to France after 1830, when his aristocratic companion, the pleasure-loving George Villiers, was enjoying himself, Bowring is usually described as working on his reports or interviewing influential persons. Meeting famous people was always an irresistible attraction to him – indeed, years later he urged his son Frederick to 'cultivate the acquaintance of authors and other eminent people' (7 November 1850). In his own earlier years he sought the friendship of Coleridge, Wordsworth, Southey and above all Byron, correspondence with whom was one of the main attractions of the post of secretary of the London Greek Committee. Later eminent acquaintances included Shelley's widow and Sir Walter Scott, whom he met in London and later visited at Abbotsford. Another celebrity – one of the many European ones whose friendship Bowring cultivated – was the French hero of the revolution in America, General Lafayette, whose estate in France Bowring visited during one of his early commercial missions. (Bowring wrote an enthusiastic account of the visit to his wife.)

On most of his visits to the continent Bowring had his album available. The Unitarian diarist, Crabb Robinson, formed an unfavourable opinion of him from the 'ostentatious *Stammbuch* he keeps, which Talfourd delivered to Wordsworth at Bowring's request for his signature'. At the meeting with Coleridge, Robinson was irritated by Bowring's obsequiousness and found him 'ostentatious of his own foreign and various connections'. Collecting the autographs of distinguished people was to remain a lifelong passion with Bowring in spite of his disapproval of people who cut the signature of celebrities, such as Byron, off their letters. In a letter to his Slav collaborator, Frantisek Celakowsky, in 1830, he requested the signatures, with a few lines of verse, of the leading Slav scholars of the day. Particularly astonishing was the episode when Bowring's Chinese opponent, Commissioner Yeh Ming-Ch'en, was captured and taken to Hong Kong in 1857. Bowring, then governor of the colony, invited the commissioner, who had outwitted him at Canton, to write in his album. Yeh replied with dignity that it was impossible to write a trivial piece of Chinese verse.

Bowring would sometimes pass on the letters of distinguished people to his acquaintances. An affectionate letter from Bentham to Bowring came into the possession of Aspland, perhaps given to the minister by Bowring to impress him with his close relations with the famous philosopher. The introduction to Bentham in August

1820 was arranged, after some delay, by Bowring's radical friend, Edward Blaquiere, an Irish naval captain who shared his enthusiasm for Spain, though their friendship was later to cool after disagreements over Greece. Blaquiere, an inveterate traveller, was aptly described by Bowring as 'a kind of wandering apostle of Benthamism'. Bentham, a bachelor, lived alone, except for his secretaries, at Queen's Square Place, Westminster, next door to his friend James Mill and did not usually like meeting strangers. But he was immediately entranced by his new disciple. As he wrote enthusiastically to his brother in France:

> What I owe to Blaquiere for himself is much, but what I owe him for Bowring is unspeakable. His useful knowledge, talent, connections, disinterestedness and philanthropy conjoined far surpasses anything I could have believed possible. He is but 28 yet there are few languages in Europe in which he could not write to the press nor does not understand ... He comes here at my beck and call and would come oftener as he lives in Hackney and cannot stay after nine. I have not yet had time to know half of what he is worth, I have scarcely yet been able to find out what it is he does not know. He is quick as lightening ... gentle as lambs are said to be and not less brave. He has one child and another coming, as happy with his wife as it is possible for mortal man to be – it is very necessary your girls should know this or they would fall in love with him and be miserable. Sure as a gun I should have him for a nephew-in-law if I could but contrive to cut the throat of that cursed woman and her brat. Sure enough she would be glad enough to cut mine for taking her husband away from her for the best part of one day in every four.

Bowring's friend Blaquiere, who was naturally inclined to be somewhat jealous of Bentham's enthusiasm for his new disciple, was assured by the philosopher that 'Bowring is in Elysium. He and I are son and father. He is one of the most extraordinary if not the most extraordinary man I ever saw in my life ... What a pity his health is so delicate and the winter in this country is scarce tolerable to him. He is the most loving creature God Almighty ever made. I

10

scold him for leaving his wife and child as he does, yet he never leaves me, he says, but in better health as well as spirits'.

This interest in Bowring was no passing whim on Bentham's part and was to last uninterrupted for the remaining 12 years of Bentham's life. Bentham was not noted for the permanency of his attachments, while he had been alone too long to be an easy companion. Moreover, far from being a cold and dispassionate reasoner of the familiar Utilitarian type, such as James Mill, Bentham's new disciple was a writer of verse translations and a member of a Christian sect. Bentham certainly laughed at Bowring's poetry, declaring his Russian volume 'a foolish sort of work . . . which he engaged in before he knew me'. And he was well aware of the exaggerated extent to which Bowring claimed a knowledge of unfamiliar languages. But this did not prevent his adding his name to the subscription lists of Bowring's verse translations. As Bentham's secretary, John Colls, was quick to point out, Bowring lost no opportunity of flattering the aged philosopher both with his tongue and with his pen, though he was not above entertaining his friends with anecdotes illustrating Bentham's eccentricity.

It would be untrue, however, to conclude that all the advantages of the friendship were on one side. Bentham received from Bowring a thousand services. Whether it was the translation of Bentham's correspondence with the liberals of Europe and Latin America, the distribution of his published works or the editing and publication of his untidy notes, such as *Observations on the Restrictive and Prohibitory System of Commerce*, which appeared in print in 1821, Bowring was always ready to put his resources as a merchant and his experience as a linguist and traveller at Bentham's disposal. Indeed, Bowring's counting-house near Cornhill became a clearing-house through which books, pamphlets and newspapers were despatched on behalf of Bentham to Spain and many other parts of the world. As Bentham facetiously declared in one of his early letters to Bowring, 'now that you have taken me under your protection, there are some hopes for me'. A daily exchange of correspondence and packages now took place between Queen's Square and Freeman's Court, Cornhill: letters from Spain for Bowring to translate, the latest information from Blaquiere to be commented on, suggestions for a new Spanish penal code to be forwarded to Madrid by Bowring's agent at Vittoria 'in the hope of saving the letters from the clutches of the creatures of French misrule'. Each package would be accompanied by a note scribbled in Bentham's untidy hand across the sheet and along the sides, with several illegible postscripts at the bottom. As Bentham admitted to Bowring in one of these notes early in 1821, 'What I have to pour in upon you, would overwhelm anybody else but you, but the shoulders of your mind are borrowed from Hercules. Monster as you are!' In addition to the political pamphlets, there were packages of a more personal nature to be despatched. Bowring undertook to arrange for plants, seeds and even livestock to be conveyed to Sir Samuel Bentham's estate in the south of France. When in December 1820 Bowring's partner, Murdoch, set off for Spain, he took with him 'numerous little packets' for Sir Samuel, as well as a letter of introduction in which Bentham assured his brother that Murdoch was 'a man in whom you may without danger repose any confidence'. Two months later Bowring himself declared his intention of revisiting Spain, if he could recall his partner home and undertook to 'fall on his knees' before Sir Samuel Bentham.

It was not, however, until July 1821, four months after the birth of his first son, John, that Bowring set out for the Continent, taking with him copies of the *Constitutional Code* and other of Bentham's treatises translated into Spanish for the edification of the liberal government now established at Madrid. He also took with him a tract on Universal Peace by the anti-slavery campaigner Thomas Clarkson and a pamphlet in Spanish denouncing slavery in Cuba. His reasons for the journey were ostensibly commercial ones, partly to sort out his own business difficulties, partly to press the claims of his old employers, Milford and Co., against the Spanish and Portuguese governments. He also had several literary projects to attend to. For several weeks he remained in Paris where he extended his acquaintance with various liberal politicians. While in the French capital, Bowring was introduced to Louis Philippe, Duke of Orleans, who received him cordially and arrangements were made for several of Bentham's works to be forwarded to the Duke's residence at Neuilly. Late in August Bowring continued his journey to the south of France where he probably paid a brief visit to Sir Samuel Bentham. Entering Spain he found 'a terrific epidemic of yellow fever' had broken out and he was delayed, not for the only time in his life, in the 'duress vile of Quarantine'. He had originally intended to go straight to Madrid but either because of the fever or in order to sort out business problems, he spent part of October with his agent at Vittoria and did not reach the capital till the following month. There he discovered that circumstances had greatly changed since the enthusiastic days of 1820, for quarrels had broken out between different factions in the government, which were rapidly leading to a condition of civil war. After nearly two months in Madrid, Bowring, whose political and commercial activities were interrupted by an 'alarming illness', abandoned plans to visit Portugal and set out for Cadiz on the first stage of his journey home, probably visiting Gibraltar where his firm still had a branch. According to *John Bull*, Bowring's journey had been undertaken mainly for the purpose of collecting his debts, in order to satisfy the demands of a large body of creditors. Finding this difficult in the disturbed condition of the country, he returned to England more seriously compromised than before. As he confessed to Bentham, 'if I were at ease as respects my commercial concerns I should be a happy creature ... I feel an excessive desire to talk with you of plans and places which fly about in my unquiet brain – bright expectations dispersed and crushed by one melancholy ever present thought'. In spite of his familiarity with the country, his literary interest and his ailing business concerns, this seems to have been the last occasion on which Bowring himself visited Spain. The collapse of the liberal regime after French intervention in 1823 rendered him *persona non grata* in Madrid. As far as is known he never returned to the Peninsula though he tried later, without success, to obtain an official appointment at Madrid when his fellow commissioner in France in the 1830s, George Villiers, became British ambassador to Spain in 1834.

Bowring's hesitation to revisit Bourbon Spain was increased by an unpleasant incident which occurred during his return from a trip to Paris late in 1822. During the year since his previous visit, several uprisings against the reactionary Bourbon government had taken place, culminating in the trial and execution of four sergeants at La Rochelle on a charge of treason. In this atmosphere of intrigue Bowring's association with the Orleanist circle developed rapidly, the visitor worming his way into the centre of events. As he wrote impressively to his family, 'several of the leading liberals have been requesting me to urge the Duke to mingle more with the liberal party and to become the rallying point of the friends of liberty. I have been made acquainted with a scheme now at work for changing

13

the government which everybody says will not last'. Leaving Paris on on 3 October in the company of Blaquiere, Bowring arrived at Calais two days later. There, 'at the moment of embarkation', he was detained by the police, who had placed him under surveillance and forced him to open his luggage. His trunk was ransacked, his person examined and 'fifteen letters, some packets and the Portuguese despatches' were taken from him besides an envelope 'containing two ridiculous songs and the account of the death of a young liberal'. The documents appeared to satisfy the police and after making his protest and handing in his passport, Bowring was allowed for the time being to leave. Three days later, however, he was suddenly arrested, conveyed to jail 'with a face much swollen and inflamed from toothache' and there confined 'in a damp and dreary apartment' where he spent a sleepless night in the company of a murderer and a forger. Next day he was taken to Boulogne where he received another examination and was 'greatly surprised' to be directed back to prison. There he remained for the next month whilst Blaquiere hurried off to England to obtain his release. In return for a tip, Bowring was allowed to use the jailor's room during the day but had to share the common cell at night 'where all crimes are blended without distinction'. Though his papers were taken from him, he was permitted to keep his writing material and was able to work on his second volume of Russian translations. Two charges had been laid against Bowring; that of complicity in a plot to rescue the four sergeants of La Rochelle by bribing the jailor and that of carrying sealed letters of a treasonable nature. Bowring stoutly denied his guilt, affirming his ignorance of the despatches he carried. Years later, however, in his recollections of the affair, he admitted that 'both accusations had, in truth, some evidence to support them', for an incriminating Bill of Exchange had been found with his name endorsed on it, while the Portuguese despatches 'announced the intended French invasion of the Peninsula'.

Meanwhile in England the affair got into the newspapers and brought into action the full resources of Bowring's family both at Hackney and Exeter, as well as efforts by Blaquiere to secure his release. Bowring's wife proposed to join her husband at Boulogne with his sister Anne and wrote to the British Ambassador at Paris seeking his assistance. Bowring's father wrote to Lant Carpenter, now minister at Lewin's Mead Chapel, Bristol, expressing his grief over the arrest of his son. In the family troubles at Exeter in later years, when he was in his old age and bordering on senility, Bowring's father seems rather a helpless figure. At this period, however, his deep concern for his son's safety is expressed in a surviving letter to Carpenter with dignity and pious resignation.

That the circumstances of my son's arrest in a foreign country has been to me and mine a heavy calamity you will easily conceive and the unprepared and unexpected manner in which the communication was made added not a little to its poignancy. It was on Sunday morning when with my family I was going to the Meeting House (indeed Mrs Bowring and my daughters had entered) that I was called aside by a friend to enquire whether I had seen the account in the public papers respecting my son. The appalling paragraph was presented to me and I leave you to conceive what must be the feelings of a parent on reading it. There is no doubt party feeling had highly coloured the report but ... the simple fact of his being arrested and imprisoned was an overwhelming grief.

After adding that Bowring's wife 'had evinced much firmness and composure of mind' and had appealed to Canning, the Foreign Secretary, and other influential people such as Lord Holland (who was one of Bowring's earliest literary patrons), he continued:

I endeavour to divest myself as much as possible of undue anxiety – it is a duty which I owe myself and those who are dearest to me and the great exemplar of human suffering has encouraged us both by precept and practice to refer ourselves under all events however afflictive to the guidance of that wisdom which cannot err and the protection of that providence which is a refuge for the sons of sorrow – the will of God be done ...

Bowring's own letters to his father and to Carpenter are less impressive, rather meriting the contemptuous comment of his brother-in-law, Tom Lewin, who came to the aid of his sister in the crisis, that 'he quite imagines himself a hero – as if any fool couldn't get into as stupid a scrape. He wrote from Boulogne that he is

15

fighting the case of millions'. 'I knew not that I was so important a personage here', Bowring wrote to his father from prison, 'I hope you will be calm and breathe no thoughts of blame for I deserve none. My arrest makes, I suppose, a great noise in England and I suppose I shall be instantly claimed by the British government . . . You must not blush now but rejoice that tried in the balance of suffering, your son was not found wanting. I shall come from these walls to your Woods and your Waters and your Green Fields – their green will be as Emeralds . . .'

In spite of this bravado – 'the act is equivalent to a declaration of war against England', he assured his father – there is no doubt that Bowring, as well as his family, was considerably alarmed by the experience, particularly as he knew there was some truth in the allegations. He told Lant Carpenter that he quite expected to go to the guillotine after a mock trial. On his return to England, Bowring was warmly greeted by Bentham, 'who seized me and pressing me to his bosom exclaimed "as the hart panteth for the water-brooks, so panteth my heart for thee my son"'. According to Bowring's second wife, he would describe this moment in his old age 'with a countenance beaming with emotion', ignoring the probable irony of Bentham's biblical utterances. How Bowring's wife and parents received him is not recorded. The incident coincided with the marriage of George Kenrick to Bowring's eldest sister, Margaret, and must have considerably clouded the occasion. It also coincided with the birth of Bowring's second son, Frederick, 'my prison son', as his father later referred to him.

After his return from France, Bowring published his version of events in the *Details of the Arrest, Imprisonment and Liberation of An Englishman*, an exercise in self-publicity which drew varying opinions on his conduct. The *Commercial Chronicle* deplored the arrest of the 'well known and elegant translator of the Russian Anthology' who was 'at night locked up with the common prisoners in a most filthy hole'. Questions were also asked in the House of Commons but, having secured his release, the government was not prepared to take any further steps on Bowring's behalf. Soon after his release Bowring published an article in the *Pamphleteer*, describing the unsatisfactory state of prisons in Spain and Portugal, as part of an attempt to press the advantages of Bentham's Panoptikon system on the Spanish Cortes. The overthrow of the liberal regime

16

in Spain prevented any further progress in the matter, but the article remains an interesting early example of Bowring's adeptness in presenting a mass of unfamiliar facts and figures in the form of a report.

2

The Young Radical in Trouble

Between 1821 and 1828 Bowring's wife gave birth to her five sons, John, Frederick, Lewin, Edgar and Charles and in the 1830s to three more daughters, Edith, Emily and Gertrude. This was an age when childbirth was a hazardous matter; all Bowring's three married sons were to lose their first wives, his sister Margaret was to die in childbirth two years after her marriage and his sister-in-law, Anne Ward, was also to die in childbirth. There is no evidence, in spite of various ailments in her later years, that Maria Bowring's health suffered from her frequent confinements, though several of these took place in difficult circumstances.

During these years of a steadily increasing family, Bowring was heavily engaged with Bentham's affairs, including the political editorship of the *Westminster Review*, founded in 1824, for which Bentham paid him a good salary. (Another Unitarian, Henry Southern, was for a time the literary editor). In spite of the hostility to Bowring of James Mill and his son and the objections of the Revd Aspland, who prophesied the *Review* would not last for six months, the journal earned a high reputation for its political articles, including its sturdy exposition of the Utilitarian philosophy, attracting some of the best writers of the day. The editorship of the *Westminster Review* was of considerable importance to Bowring, as in spite of disputes with contributors, and the extent of time it took him away from his business responsibilities, it gave him an enhanced status in the literary world, adding to his reputation as a foreign verse translator. It also provided a platform in its early years for the activities of the London Greek Committee.

The collapse of the liberal regime in Spain almost coincided with the rising in Greece against the Turks, and Bowring, Blaquiere and many other young radicals hastened to transfer their enthusiasm to the new cause. As secretary of the London Greek Committee, formed in 1823 to send supplies of money and equipment – as well as Utilitarian literature – to assist the struggling Greeks, Bowring played a prominent part in the enterprise. It enabled him to send obsequious letters to his hero, Lord Byron, who, as is well known, went out to Greece to fight for the cause of Greek freedom. Bowring's first connection with Greece was probably in 1821, for in August that year two Greeks from Paris called at Bentham's house on Bowring's recommendation with some pamphlets for the philosopher. In November Bowring assisted an Italian philhellene, Count Palma, in the formation of a Greek committee in Madrid. When early in 1822 the proclamation of a Greek Constitution was made, Bowring wrote to the provisional government in Greece, offering his services. Several months later a delegate from the provisional government, which had decided to raise a loan in Europe, arrived at Madrid. This delegate, Andreas Louriottes, a Greek merchant and friend of the rebel leader, Mavrocordatos, got in touch with Blaquiere and was advised by him that London was a better place to obtain money than anywhere on the continent. In February 1823, soon after Bowring's release from prison, Louriottes arrived in London where he met Bowring and other supporters and agreed to return immediately to Greece in company with Blaquiere in order to prepare a report on the state of the country and secure the appointment of official agents to handle negotiations for a loan.

The arrival of a Greek patriot in England provided the incentive for the English philhellenes to act and on 28 February a meeting of 25 friends of Greece was held in London. This brought together many of those who were to be concerned with the cause of Greek independence, including three radical members of parliament with whom Bowring was to have a particularly close acquaintance, John Cam Hobhouse, the friend of Byron, Joseph Hume and Edward Ellice. A committee was set up with Bowring as secretary to consider the best means of promoting the cause of the Greeks. It was decided to open a subscription list to provide funds for equipping an expedition to the Morea. It was also decided, on Hobhouse's suggestion, to get into touch with Lord Byron in Italy with the purpose of inviting the famous poet to represent the 'London Greek Committee' in Greece.

On 14 March 1823 Bowring sent Byron notice of the committee's offer, accompanied by a flattering private letter. Unfortunately the letter was directed to Calais in the mistaken belief that Byron was returning to England and it was not until May that it reached the poet, who informed Bowring of his willingness 'to go up into the Levant in person'. Meanwhile Blaquiere had arrived in Greece and in an enthusiastic letter to Bowring pointed out the political and commercial possibilities of the country. 'I shall write to Gibraltar tomorrow', he declared, 'to urge M [Murdoch] to send up some goods. There is a tremendous opening here for anybody that has a little money to spare'. He impressed upon the Greek provisional government the necessity for raising money in England, secured the appointment of Louriottes and John Orlandos, a deputy of the 'National Assembly', as agents for the loan and hastened back home, as enthusiastic now for Greece as he had previously been for Spain.

Whilst Blaquiere was in Greece making arrangements for a loan, Bowring was busy in London trying to arouse enthusiasm on behalf of Greece. Between March and May 1823 he wrote hundreds of letters to possible supporters, urging people to accept membership of the London Greek Committee. In spite of his zeal, however, only 70 names had been obtained by the time the first public meeting of the committee took place in May. When it came to securing subscribers, the position was even less satisfactory as most people were unwilling to open their purses without some guarantee that their money would be wisely spent. As Bowring admitted to Byron, the committee had not made the progress he expected. 'The Spanish cause has absorbed attention', he explained, 'and we begin to fear unworthily'. In spite of these disappointments the committee pursued its campaign with energy, organising public exhibitions including 'the sensational ascent of a balloon on novel principles'. By October over £7000 had been raised, but compared with the success of philhellenes across the Atlantic, this was a very modest achievement. With the money thus provided, the committee was able to send material to Greece in the care of an artillery expert. But the discovery that this included printing presses and mathematical instruments, as well as arms and ammunition, roused Byron to fury. 'The supplies of the committee are all excellent of their kind', he wrote to Bowring, 'but occasionally hardly practical enough in the present state of Greece ... we must conquer first and plan afterwards'. It was essential, he insisted, that if effective military help was to be given to the already disunited Greek forces, a loan should be floated as soon as possible. This appeal for money was not lost upon the committee, who were well aware of the need to supplement subscriptions by a loan. As Bowring wrote to Hobhouse in December, 'bad as the state of things are, I would engage to secure the Greeks a loan of £600,000 by tomorrow morning if anybody invested with powers were here. I am sure of this – a friend of mine would give me £150,000'.

In January 1824 uncertainty was at last brought to an end by the arrival in London of the two agents, Orlandos and Louriottes, appointed to negotiate the loan. They immediately opened negotiations with the London Greek Committee. Agreement was soon reached and in February a contract was signed for a loan of £800,000 on the security of part of the soil of Greece. A sinking fund was placed under the control of Hume and Ellice, who, together with the firm of Loughnan and Son, were to act as contractors on behalf of the committee. On 21 February the Greek loan was officially launched at a banquet in the City and a few days later it was floated at the rate of 59. At first, all went well. Prospectuses appeared in the leading newspapers and within a few days the loan was heavily oversubscribed. Bowring, who secured bonds to the nominal value of £25,000 – and taken a handsome commission for his part in arranging the loan – was delighted. 'The terms of the loan were much better than we could expect', he wrote to Colonel Leicester Stanhope, who was in Greece, 'it was wonderful to see how many offers were made of money'.

Early in March, however, he became involved in a quarrel with the two Greek deputies, who wrote to Bentham accusing Bowring of having tricked them over the loan contract. This concerned the detailed instructions for the disposal of the loan which, as Bowring explained to Bentham, if employed for purposes specified by the two deputies, would have 'alarmed the lenders for it trumpeted forth the dissentions of the Greeks'. Both parties continued to put their view to Bentham, who was given an occasion to exercise the prudence and benevolence of his own philosophy. After trying in vain to arrange a settlement, he advised the deputies to accept the situation if they wanted to get the money. This Orlandos and Louriottes reluctantly agreed to do. But in spite of many protestations of friendship they continued to house a deep resentment against Bowring. Later, when Bentham tried to persuade the deputies to recommend

Bowring as Greek Consul in London, they did all they could to urge the Greek government not to have anything to do with him. As the value of Greek stock began to fall, the personal distrust between Bowring and the deputies became greater. Each party suspected the other of allowing private interest to come before the needs of Greece. According to Orlandos and Louriottes the Greek Committee meant in reality one or two persons such as Bowring and Loughnan, who were trying to enrich themselves at the expense of the Greeks. According to Bowring, the deputies were trying to make themselves independent of control by the committee, in order to use their funds for political intrigues in Greece.

In May 1824 all this tension was brought to a head by news of the death of Byron at Missolonghi, shortly before the arrival of Blaquiere with the first instalment of the loan. This disaster came as a great shock to those who were trying to restore confidence in the loan, for it had been Byron's name which had persuaded many people to invest their money in Greek stock. In these circumstances it is not surprising that a meeting between Bowring and the deputies was a most unpleasant one. According to the deputies (who wrote an account of the affair to one of their supporters in Greece), Bowring was now determined to ruin the loan because he could no longer exploit it to his own advantage. He hoped to make necessary a new loan which would be carried through by 'more docile' Greek agents, so that he could devise fresh plans to enrich himself. It is true that Bowring was urging the replacement of Orlandos and Louriottes on the Greek government. As he wrote to Hobhouse in July 1824:

I have had so much annoyance with these Greek affairs ... that I have determined to retire from the Committee as secretary at least. I cannot obtain from Orlando and Luriottis even the civility of an answer to my letters. – I will write no more. A man who has written three or four thousand letters to serve a cause (as I have done) and then by way of reward cannot get a civil word from the representatives of that cause must have a passion for being so scorned if he bear it long.

As the situation deteriorated Bowring found himself held responsible for many of the disasters which had occurred. The deputies attacked him as an enemy of Greece, the bond-holders blamed him for their

22

disappointing investments in the loan and the Tory press gleefully calculated the fortunes he had made at the expense of the Greeks and the bond-holders, though his real financial position had been weakened by unwise speculation and neglect of his business affairs. As he admitted to a correspondent at Corfu, 'The loan is in a terrible state and I, who have almost found the half, am accused of having . . . deceived the English people although I have suffered more than anyone else in this affair having lost a fortune in obtaining and upholding the credit of the Greek government'. Faced with financial disaster, Bowring brought pressure on the deputies to relieve him of his shares at a price higher than the current market value of Greek stock – one of several somewhat dubious financial manoeuvres in which he became involved at this period.

These actions were to rebound on him two years later when, following an almost equally disastrous second Greek loan, in which Bowring and the Greek committee played little part, further reverses in Greece brought the mismanagement of both loans into the open. Bowring attempted to justify the actions of his committee and himself in an article in the *Westminster Review* in 1826, defending the management of the first loan and attacking the handling of the second, in which the two deputies had again been involved. After two angry meetings of shareholders of Greek stock had been held at which Bowring and a resuscitated Greek Committee had tried to justify themselves, *The Times* entered the fray, publishing the full story of Bowring's financial transactions with the deputies in 1824 and giving an account of similar shady conduct on the part of Hume and Ellice. These accounts were quickly confirmed by Louriottes, who may have provided the newspaper with its information in the first place, though rumours were already circulating in the City. The *Times* revelations created an immense stir even for an age which was hardened to financial scandals, and political opponents of the philhellenes took full advantage of the opportunity to point out how the champions of the Greeks had behaved. William Cobbett devoted several issues of his *Political Register* to an examination of the 'Greek Pie' into which 'Burdett, Hobhouse, Ellice, Hume and Bowring have been cramming their fingers'. Bowring's account of the first loan, which, he said, had given him a great deal of trouble because of the divisions amongst the Greeks and the dispute with the deputies, was not considered very convincing; nor was his explanation that some sharp

23

practice over the manipulation of Greek stock was due to a family sorrow, the death of his eldest sister, Margaret, 'when the mind is not responsible for its own acts'. 'Bowring', sneered Cobbett, 'talks fine – but he will find that we shall want something more than fine talk to satisfy us that the Greek bondholders and the Greeks themselves have had fair play at the hands of this patriot'.

The radicals were greatly disturbed by the indiscretions of the Greek Committee and many letters were sent to Bentham, warning him against Bowring and pointing out the bad reputation he held even amongst foreign liberals as a result of his financial activities over the Greek loan. Bentham, however, refused to listen to these detractors for, as Francis Place, who once described Bowring contemptuously as a 'wild, poetical surface man', noted in his diary, 'Bowring gives much time to him and takes him out with him now and then and for this Bentham undoubtedly owes something to Bowring. Bowring also panders to him, is his toad eater, and can therefore command him and ... to deprive him of Bowring without substituting someone in his stead would, if it could be done, make him unhappy'. Bowring himself later recorded his gratitude for Bentham's support 'through a period of my existence in which I was steeped in poverty and overwhelmed with slander ... I was calumniated on every side and the calumnies were addressed in multitudes to my protector'. Bentham, indeed, was not the only person to stand by Bowring at this time. Quite apart from members of his own family, whose reactions are not recorded, many of his co-religionists rallied to his support. The Unitarian minister, Joseph Hunter, noted in his diary that 'the Greek business' brought Bowring's name 'much before the public and latterly not in the most agreeable manner but there were those who thought that he came well out of the scrape into which the *Times* had brought him'. The 'Greek Pie', however, was going to haunt Bowring for the rest of his days, particularly during election campaigns and in the years of his unpopularity in China. Greece, with its unhappy memories, was one of the few European countries which he never seems to have visited, nor, in spite of plans to do so, did he ever publish a volume of Greek verse translations.

Throughout these years of difficulty and disappointment, Bowring was still maintaining a large and complex correspondence over his foreign verse translations. This sometimes involved him in the disputes and jealousies of continental scholars. His work reached a peak of activity during the 1820s which lasted until the end of the decade, when public enthusiasm for the 'Songs of the People' went out of fashion and Bowring's verses became a target for ridicule in some of the journals, such as *Fraser's Magazine*. In addition to a second volume of Russian poets, partly written, according to Bowring, in prison in Boulogne, and a book of translations from the *Ancient Poetry and Romances of Spain* and some translations of German verse, Bowring, with the help of a long line of continental collaborators and correspondents, produced Dutch, Polish, Serbian, Magyar and Bohemian translations into English in volume form, as well as translations from an even larger variety of languages. These verses appeared in journals such as the *Westminster Review*, the *London Magazine* and the *Foreign Quarterly Review*. Virtually all Bowring's volumes of verse translations, which he published at his own expense and sold, as time moved on, with increasing difficulty, were prefaced by an impressive display of honorary memberships of various foreign learned societies, together with a dedication to some prominent royal or diplomatic figure. In all his volumes of verse, Bowring, an ardent supporter of the Peace Society, claimed to have a moral as well as a practical purpose, each new volume adding 'another link to the chains of social and friendly feeling which should bind man to his fellows'. 'I have never', he wrote on one occasion, 'left the ark of my country but with the wish to return to it bearing fresh olive branches of peace and fresh garlands of poetry'. A less unctious comment on his own verse translations was scribbled by Bowring on the back of a letter from the Greek deputies:

> I'm the John Bowring who wrote the Anthologies,
> And – if there's truth in the laurelled one's strain,
> I have a right – without any apologies,
> I – who have scribbled – to scribble again.

It was during his years as a literary celebrity that a fine portrait of Bowring, 'linguist and traveller', was painted by the artist, John King. The painting bears out the comment of the American journalist John Neal, who was staying with Bentham in 1826 and, for a time, was quite friendly with Bowring, that he had 'a refined, intellectual face'. It was one of several paintings or engravings made during Bowring's youth. A bronze medallion of Bowring's head was cast at Paris in

1832 by P. D. d'Angers (reproduced on the front of *Autobiographical Recollections*) a 'masterpiece', so Bowring assured his wife. The King painting was donated to the National Portrait Gallery by the second Lady Bowring a few years before her death, where it can still be seen.

Bowring's reputation as a versifier did not only depend on his foreign translations. In 1823 he published *Matins and Vespers: with Hymns and Occasional Devotional Pieces*, freely based on a German version of daily devotions by Dr Witzchel. This was republished in enlarged editions on several occasions and became probably the most widely used of all Bowring's works, particularly with non-conformist congregations. (Even today some of Bowring's hymns are still sung). The first edition, dedicated to Lant Carpenter, gave Bowring some embarrassment, as Carpenter disapproved of some of the contents and Bowring was obliged to change the dedication to the aged Mrs Barbauld. Bowring published another collection of hymns in 1825 and composed devotional verse for Unitarian periodicals throughout his life. Shortly after his death his widow published *A Memorial Volume of Sacred Poetry by the Late Sir John Bowring*. The early volumes of sacred verse, which coincided in time with Bowring's more dubious activities over Greek scrip and exotic verse translations, brought comfort to many, and Bowring sometimes received letters of gratitude. As he wrote to an unnamed acquaintance in 1826 (possibly connected with the New Gravel Pit Congregation):

> I return you (with many thanks) the affecting letter of Mr Montgomery. To add something to human happiness is a great privilege – it is *indeed* great to have added one sweet drop to the cup of religious peace and joy – to diminish the suffering and sorrow of a single human being is something – but to have smoothed and solaced the dying hour is *much*. I am not vain, I hope – nor proud – but Mr M's letter is one of many which have most richly rewarded me for having published that little (but imperfect) book. I have planted my blade of grass while others have filled gardens – and fertilized provinces – and reared up forests.

During these years of personal and political disaster, Bowring somehow found time to play an active part in the British and Foreign

Unitarian Association, established by Aspland mainly to campaign for the repeal of the Test Acts. Bowring himself produced an open letter to Canning urging repeal. In 1827 Bowring succeeded Fox as 'foreign secretary' of the association and this gave him the opportunity to establish communication with prominent foreign Unitarians, such as the American preacher, Revd William Channing, and the leaders of the Hindu liberal movement in India, including Ram Mohun Roy. He also wrote reports for the *Monthly Repository* on religious developments on the continent and in Britain, including the repeal of the Test Acts in 1828 and what Bowring described as 'the truly great and glorious Catholic Emancipation Act of 1829' – a landmark in religious toleration which was to have profound effects on his own family. In spite of his frequent absences abroad after 1830, he continued to play a prominent part in Unitarian affairs, publishing articles in the religious journals and addressing meetings. After his election to Parliament in 1835 he particularly acquired, as one of the few Unitarian MPs, an enhanced authority. How regularly his family continued to attend the Hackney chapel after the move from London Fields is not certain, but Bowring's brother-in-law, Samuel Lewin, remained a member of the executive committee of the New Gravel Pit Congregation.

With so many political and literary activities to occupy his attention, it is not surprising that Bowring's business affairs suffered and that he became increasingly involved in debt. As early as 1823 *John Bull* advised him to 'turn his wits to the liquidation of his own debts rather than to the emancipation of the Spanish people'. Bowring, however, in spite of increasing penury, tried, as the John King portrait suggests, to keep up appearances. 'You have no conception', drily observed Tom Lewin to his other brother-in-law, Thomas Ward, 'what a great man Bowring is. He is at present about to pay two thirds of his debts and as he is only two or three or four or five thousand pounds behindhand in the world, is going to keep a horse; but I believe he would keep a carriage till he arrives at zero. He sported a court dress when he went to the Mansion House dinner. Mr Piper saw him there and says he was a glorious quiz with bagwig and sword, chin well stuck-up and eyes peeping out beneath his spider-leg, blue steel spectacles'. Unwise investments in Greek stock and South American mines, together with extravagance in maintaining the style of a City merchant and a member of the Fishmongers

Company, helped to bring about the disaster which, not for the only time in his life, disrupted Bowring's family and broke up his home. Not much is known about the final days of Bowring and Co. and the unfortunate Murdoch. Harriet Martineau's intense dislike of Bowring may well derive from some part played in the collapse of the Martineau family enterprise at Norwich at the end of the decade. 'Neglecting trade', wrote the *Athenaeum* many years later, 'trade neglected him and the profits of his first seven years as a merchant were spent in improvident speculation'.

By late 1827 the collapse of Bowring and Co. was complete. 'You know, of course, that the storm has burst', wrote Bowring to Fox (and in very similar words to Hobhouse), 'my home abandoned – my wife and children dispersed and I am on the way to other climes ... I have now with half a dozen little ones to start anew in life'. This was, indeed, hardly an exaggeration. Bowring's eldest son, John, was sent to his mother's relations at Sheffield, where he later attended a Unitarian school at Norton. Frederick and Lewin were sent to their grandfather at Exeter and were to remain there throughout their childhood, becoming pupils at a private school at Mount Radford on the old Baring estate, close to Larkbear. Bowring and his wife with Maria and the infant Edgar migrated to Heidelberg, partly to avoid Bowring's creditors but mainly because Bowring, with Bentham's strong support, was now seeking the professorship of literature at the newly established and Utilitarian-inspired London University and hoped to improve his chances by associating himself with well-known German scholars. He also had plans – later abandoned – to visit some of his Slav and Magyar verse collaborators at Vienna. After a few weeks at Heidelberg and Bonn, Bowring continued his university tour to the Netherlands and then returned to England in 1828, where he took up residence with Bentham. Bowring's university ambitions were, however, to be frustrated as he faced the opposition of many powerful supporters of the new institution, such as Henry Brougham, who disliked his influence over Bentham. Bowring, who believed his Unitarianism had caused his rejection, wrote an angry letter to the *Morning Herald*, protesting at the violation of the secular principles of the new institution, which, he believed, was already coming under Anglican influence. It is doubtful, however, whether unorthodox religious opinions played a major part in his failure, as there were enough opponents on the university council to make sure that his candidature should not be taken seriously.

Disappointed in his plans for an academic career and still greatly in need of money, Bowring now tried to secure employment as a member of a government commission examining the Public Accounts; a curious action in view of his well-known radicalism, his recent commercial disasters and his unsavoury reputation over the Greek loans. The chairman of the commission, however, Sir Henry Parnell, was a follower of Bentham, and another prominent member, the Master of the Mint, J. C. Herries, had connections with the Baring family of Exeter, close neighbours of the Bowrings. Although the Prime Minister, the Duke of Wellington, would not permit the employment of 'such a damned radical', Bowring was eventually allowed to visit the Netherlands as an unpaid commissioner, receiving only his expenses, in order to prepare a review of the Dutch system of public accounts – a review which soon got him into trouble with the Dutch royal family, who regarded his enquiries as intrusive. It was during one of his visits to the Netherlands in 1829 that Bowring received an honorary doctorate for his services to Dutch literature from the University of Groningen, an honour which the Dutch must have later regretted in view of Bowring's enthusiastic support for Belgian independence after the rift with the Dutch part of the Netherlands in 1830. Henceforth Bowring was to be known to most of his acquaintances as 'The Doctor'.

In this trail of disasters, Bowring had one important success. In spite of the opposition of James Mill and his son, who tried to persuade him to resign after the Greek loan affair, on the grounds that the review could not afford a paid editor, Bowring (who at first pretended to agree with the Mills) succeeded in retaining his position on the *Westminster Review*, which now passed from Bentham into the ownership of Colonel Perronet Thompson. Thompson, an example of a familiar type of the period, the radical ex-soldier, (the philhellenes, Colonel Leicester Stanhope and Colonel Groves Jones were others), was to own and largely write the *Westminster Review* for about eight years, though it never recovered the prestige of its early days. In spite of efforts by Joseph Hume and Place to get them to do so, neither James Mill nor his son were prepared to contribute again to the review whilst Bowring remained editor. Thompson was to become a friend of Bowring and his family, sharing Bowring's enthusiasm for Free Trade and 'general liberalism'. Indeed he nearly became father-in-law to Bowring's son Edgar during the 1850s before a rift over the *Arrow* affair in China brought the long friendship to an end. Under Thompson and Bowring the *Westminster Review* became more sympathetic than in Bentham's day to works of the imagination. Tennyson's *Poems Chiefly Lyrical* was enthusiastically reviewed in 1830 and Scott's works were treated with particular favour, as Bowring was seeking the famous novelist's collaboration in his Scandinavian verse project. Bowring had obtained a Czech translation of Scott's *Lady of the Lake* from his Bohemian collaborator, Celakovsky, and used this to attract Sir Walter's interest.

By late 1828, in spite of his *Westminster Review* salary and some literary sources of income, Bowring's financial situation was desperate enough for a group of friends, including Hume, Ellice and Colonel Groves Jones, together with some of Bowring's fellow Unitarians, to organise in strict confidence a fund to save Bowring's private possessions from confiscation. His principal private creditor was James Morrison, the 'Napoleon of shopkeepers', who made a fortune in retail trade. Any money left over after the discharge of Bowring's private debts was, according to the terms of the arrangement, 'preserved as a means of supply to Mrs Bowring – whenever she may be distressed – or as a means of giving present education to those children that may now require it. The furniture generally is very little more but what is essential to the uses of the family, the books chiefly are requisite for Mr Bowring's literary pursuits'. How much money was raised by the generosity of Bowring's friends, to what use it was actually put and whether any of it was eventually repaid, is unknown.

After her return from Germany, Bowring's wife, who was expecting her fifth child (Charles), had taken up residence with friends at Hackney, (Miss Gibson, Tryon Place, is given as the address on a letter to her from Bowring), presumably with her daughter, Maria, and the infant Edgar. Maria, perhaps, acted as nursemaid to her younger brother at this period. Bowring was attempting, not very successfully, to equip Bentham's 'garden house' at Queen's Square as a residence for his whole family. His movements in these months of family dispersal are not easy to trace, Bowring himself being sometimes at Queen's Square, sometimes at Larkbear, several times in the Netherlands and once in Denmark, seeking contacts for his projected Scandinavian volume. The London part of the family were probably reunited late in 1828 when Bowring took up residence at 7 North Place, Gray's Inn Lane, and were certainly together when he moved to nearby Millman Street. It was not, however, until 1831, when his fortunes had begun to improve, that he and his family were able to move into No. 1 Queen's Square, after James Mill, who had quarrelled with Bentham, had left the premises. Here Bowring and his family were to remain until his departure for China nearly twenty years later.

The move to Queen's Square made it easier for Bowring to keep an eye on Bentham, whose memoirs he was recording with the help of Bentham's secretaries. Bowring was now sharing Bentham's confidence with the lawyer, Edwin Chadwick. They were both trying to persuade the old man to make a final settlement of his will, of which Bowring was desperately anxious to become executor. The move to Queen's Square also brought Bowring in closer proximity both to parliament and to the offices of public administration from which, with Bentham's support, he was already seeking employment.

At Queen's Square Bowring, in spite of his penury, resumed his evening receptions for political and literary acquaintances. One of these occasions was described by Charles MacFarlane, a writer of travel books and other literary exercises. He was accompanied by the poet, Thomas Moore, the biographer of Byron, who had already crossed swords with Bowring over the Greek loan affair. MacFarlane, who wrote his memoirs many years later, when Bowring was governor of Hong Kong and he himself was living in poverty and ill health, was by no means well disposed either to Bowring's politics or to his literary judgement, a book of his having been adversely criticised in the *Westminster Review*. Bowring's 'entertainment', he wrote, 'must have been cheap to his purse but I fancy ... very costly to the patience of his guests. It was a tedious, desolating affair full of foreigners and political refugees from all countries ... and the agreeable pastime was to hear the Doctor talking Magyar with a Hungarian, Slavonic with a Pole, German with a German and Spanish, Portuguese, Swedish, Danish and Dutch with representatives of these nations ... I never saw such a display of vanity and never heard such volubility. The Doctor was one continuous torrent of talk. His foreigners, as in duty bound, turned up their eyes, clapped their hands and expressed astonishment and enthusiastic admiration'. MacFarlane met 'Dr Boring' again at Lytton Bulwer's dinner party, when 'before the soup was off the table, Boring took the lead of the talk and he kept it. How the two Bulwers stood it all, I could not imagine'.

In 1828 Bowring's mother had been taken seriously ill and he was obliged to make frequent visits to Exeter, where his two young sons were now living. A number of letters to his wife at Hackney have survived from this time, which give a rare glimpse of Bowring as father and of his sons, Frederick and Lewin, as young children.

> On entering the passage I met a ruddy faced stout fellow – who I accosted – but who stared at me and he was followed by another who stared too but at last moved forward and said 'why that is my papa' and then master Lewin came forward too and I got a kiss from both. Lewin is much changed. He is grown exceedingly stout – his hair has lost its curls and he does not speak plainly tho' very prettily. He is a prodigious favourite with everyone. He talks about Hackney and you but not with very distinct recollections. As to Fritz he is, I think – very intelligent – very talkative and loud voiced – but not louder voiced (according to authentic evidence) that when he came.

In another letter:

> The boys are brown as berries. I shall earnestly hope that either in Bentham's garden house or elsewhere we shall soon be together again – the *tedium vitae* grows on me daily – and no one knows what waves of bitterness are even now rushing up and down within me ... and what I wish – but I wish ever to be yours. I mean never to forget *you* – Kiss all the little ones – and write.

When Bowring's mother died in October 1828, the boys 'showed nothing but an affectionate interest – fancied she was asleep – and Fritz asked whether she would ever be well again – and Lewin whether she had a house in heaven. You will suppose what is most true, that in the present state of my mind, I have more than ever need of you'. (A much more pious account of the boys' reactions to their grandmother's death is given in *Autobiographical Recollections*.) In a letter of July 1830, Bowring urged his wife to join him at Exeter.

I do not think my father would have liked all the children to be here – he would have thought the noise and confusion too great – but if Maria returns – and you like to leave her and Charles – I am sure you will have a cordial welcome here and we would return together. I sit in the summer house the live long day – not having taken one walk or ride into the country. But the landscape is lovelier than ever and the garden more flowers. My father is well – but I think Anne's health very delicate. The boys are a good deal altered – Fritz is becoming very noisy and boyishly manly. Lewin is very much grown and is more obviously so contrasted with Edgar. The children here are now taught to think and to speak of us – to put your name above every other – to pray for us – and to look towards us. Their life is happiness itself – as well it may be.

A number of boyhood letters, carefully written, faultlessly spelt and mostly couched in questions, from Frederick to his mother have also survived. 'When will Papa come down again?' he wrote in one of the earliest of them in 1828. 'I am watching for him nearly every day'. (In a later letter) 'When is Edgar coming down? I do so wish to see him and I daresay he will be very glad to see Lewin who sends his love to Papa and a kiss to you . . . How does John like his new school, Mamma? What is he learning?' 'I wonder which has most vigour now, John or I?' he enquired when he was ten, 'it will be a great pleasure to play with him. Doubtless we shall be capital friends and I suppose Edgar will be Lewin's and I dare say we shall all be allied together'. Both boys were much influenced by their two intellectual aunts, to whom – more perhaps than to Mount Radford School – is due the somewhat precocious tone which appears in Frederick's letters as he gets older, while their uncle Charles, who seems to have possessed little of his elder brother's intense ambitions and was at that time working with his father in the family cloth business, took the boys shooting, fishing and walking on the moors, an activity which remained a pleasure to Frederick throughout his long life. Both boys picked up many school prizes, Frederick at 13 receiving Babbage's *Economy of Manufactures*, 'which is I dare say very useful though I have not yet read any of it', while Lewin was given two volumes on *The Restoration of Herculaneum and Pompei*. A year later Frederick obtained from his mother a copy of Hind's

Analytical Principles of Algebra for school use and received several more prizes including 'a splendid Greek book'. 'My library . . . is rapidly increasing in size and elegance every year', he assured his mother in 1837, when he was 15 and about to become a boarder. 'I think you said that we should come to London at Midsummer . . . I shall be very glad to see you again, as I have not seen you, sister, Charles and the little ones for some time. I suppose Edgar has gone to school as usual . . . How does Gertrude get on? I suppose I must no longer call her baby. I wish very much to see her again'.

3

The Radical Doctor

The year 1830 stands out as a landmark in Bowring's life. The July Revolution in France, followed in the autumn by the formation of a Whig government in Britain, not only made it possible for Bowring to visit the country from which he had been banned since 1823 but enabled him at last to secure employment as paid secretary to Sir Henry Parnell's Commission on the Public Accounts. This appointment led to Bowring's detailed investigation of the accountancy systems of both France and the Netherlands and was followed by an investigation into commercial relations between England and France, seeking a reduction of French tariffs on British goods. These appointments, made by the new Vice-President of the Board of Trade, Charles Poulett Thomson, a former business acquaintance of Bowring's and an admirer of Bentham, were well suited to Bowring with his facility at languages, his skill in amassing facts and figures (he was a founder member of the newly formed London Statistical Society) and his adeptness at obtaining access to persons of all grades and persuasions, from Louis Philippe downwards. But by no means all the Whigs were enthusiastic about his appointment. According to the diarist, George Greville, the appointment of Bowring, 'a theorist and a jobber, deeply implicated in the Greek Fire', was arranged by Thomson 'to have a creature of his own on the commission'. Bowring's colleague on the French commercial mission, young George Villiers, was warned against him by some of his aristocratic friends. Nevertheless they became, for a time, close companions, Bowring assiduously cultivating Villiers' friendship.

Bowring was now to be frequently away from his family for long periods, though, as at the celebrations in Paris in 1830, when he bore a message of congratulations from English radicals, he was sometimes accompanied by his wife or, in later years, by one of his older sons.

35

Even when in his own country, he was often away from home, seeking a seat in the reformed parliament for the industrial town of Blackburn and when this failed, as radical member for the City of London. In addition to all his other concerns, the illness and death of Bentham in 1832, who, we are told, died in Bowring's arms after the latter's hurried return from Blackburn, was followed – after the macabre ritual of Bentham's dissection – by a long and bitter dispute with the philosopher's nephew over his will. In accordance with this Bentham had left Bowring his papers and a sum of money towards their publication. 'I can hardly find time and thought for any person or thing but our venerable sage', he wrote to Chadwick from France as Bentham lay dying. After long delay and much angry correspondence, the legal dispute over Bentham's will was settled in Bowring's favour and he was able to proceed with the formidable task of publishing Bentham's works. In the cruel words of the *Blackburn Alfred*, 'after sticking to the good philosopher like a leech in the hope of securing a fat legacy at his death . . . the old gentleman . . . bequeathed the learned Doctor the copyright of some of his musty manuscripts . . . Polyglot, however, would have greatly preferred the money'.

The enfranchisement of industrial cities in the midlands and north, with their new electorate under the 'ten-pound householder' vote of manufacturers and merchants, provided an opportunity for radicals like Bowring to seek a seat in parliament without incurring the heavy expenses involved in fighting an election in one of the older boroughs. This opportunity was anticipated by the radicals before the Reform Bill became law; in March 1831, when the Whig Home Secretary, Lord John Russell, introduced into the Commons his first proposal for reform, a Parliamentary Candidates Society was formed by Place for the purpose of returning 'fit and proper' Members to the reformed House. It had been Bentham's desire, in his last years, to see his favourite disciple enter parliament, where he could advocate those measures of reform to which Bentham had dedicated his life; and Bowring had been one of the first 'fit and proper' candidates proposed for election. In April 1831 Bentham wrote an eloquent recommendation of Bowring to the reformers of Lancashire and accompanied this with a private letter to the Manchester radical Archibald Prentice, suggesting Bowring's adoption by the city, which would shortly be receiving representation. Prentice, who had

36

expressed a preference for Colonel Thompson as candidate, on the grounds that his pamphlets had made him 'known to the persons likely to be electors', was assured by Bentham that Bowring's familiarity with Utilitarian principles, 'fluency in speech' and 'high place in the estimation of the present administration' made him a more suitable choice than the Colonel, though he agreed it would be a 'sad mortification' if the success of one of his disciples depended on the sacrifice of the other. The matter was further discussed when Prentice visited Bentham shortly before his illness and was assured by the philosopher that 'it was a great mistake to suppose that Bowring's literature unfitted him for practical business' as his work for the Public Accounts Commission proved. No immediate decision had been made, however, for Russell's reform proposal encountered greater opposition than the radicals expected and it had required another year of political activity before the Reform Bill finally became law.

With the passing of the Act in June 1832, it became clear that an election under the new franchise would be held as soon as voting lists had been prepared and Bowring took immediate steps to secure himself a constituency. At first his hopes still centred upon Manchester, but in April he transferred his efforts to the newly enfranchised city of Blackburn on the advice of the Manchester Unitarian and liberal, Richard Potter, who had recommended Bowring to the reformers of Manchester's northern neighbour. It was Bowring's first acquaintance with Blackburn and he was anxious to introduce himself as soon as possible to his prospective constituents. At the end of May, while Bentham lay dying, Bowring paid a hurried visit to the city, accompanied by Potter, and issued his official address to the electors. Speaking on 31 May before the Bull Inn to a large gathering which included many non-voters, he assured his hearers that he would be the first to demand an extension of popular rights if 'the narrow concession of the ten-pound householder vote' proved insufficient to procure good and cheap government. 'I pledge myself', he promised, 'that I will come to you punctually and annually and give account of my conduct – that I will record every vote I give for that purpose and that I will resign my trust, if I have not fulfilled the pledges I have given, for in such a case I would be unworthy to represent free men in the great senate of my country'. 'Wherever there is misery', he added, 'it is the duty of the government to remove it and wherever there is happiness, it is equally encumbent on the government to increase it. It is bound to look with a paternal eye on all classes of the people as the Great Being does who . . . dispenses his blessings without distinctions of person'. This speech, with its Utilitarian and Unitarian echoes, gained Bowring much popularity in Blackburn. When in July he paid a second visit to the city, accompanied by two distinguished Polish expatriates, he was given an enthusiastic welcome.

But in spite of Bowring's popularity with the disenfranchised masses, it soon became clear that his victory would not be an easy one. His three rivals were all persons of local influence, determined to prove that Bowring's 'atheism' and 'republicanism' unfitted him for the representation of a city to which he was a complete stranger. Their opposition to Bowring was strengthened by the appearance of a newspaper, the *Blackburn Alfred* which, in contrast to the liberal *Blackburn Gazette*, hardly let a week pass without some attack on Bowring's political reputation and personal character. These included frequent references to the Greek loan scandals, which *The Times* had resuscitated in June by calling on Bowring to 'explain the circumstances of the Greek Loan by which the cause of Liberty was so materially affected some few years ago'. When, late in the autumn, the time of the election drew near, the *Alfred* excelled itself by serialising weekly the entire *Times* correspondence under the heading: 'Greek Loan Reminiscences, or Tracts in the life of those burning hot patriots and disinterested financiers Joseph Hume and John Bowring Esq.'. It was clear, as Thompson assured Bowring, that victory in an election which aroused such personal antagonisms would be a 'hard-won game.'

Bowring had spent the autumn in France and it was not until 3 December, barely a week before the election, that he arrived in Blackburn. Although the walls were placarded with bills urging the electors to 'Vote for Bowring and Liberty!', the excitement of the summer had considerably subsided. On the night before the actual nomination he received an unpleasant indication of the feelings of some of his opponents when a large stone was flung into the bedroom in which he was sleeping and 'missed his head by only two or three inches'. Next morning Bowring presented himself with the three other candidates at the field where the nomination was to take place. (These were the days of 'Eatanswill'-style open hustings before

38

the introduction of the secret ballot). There, after an address by each candidate, a show of hands was taken and a majority was given in favour of Bowring and the other liberal candidate. (Most constituencies returned two members to parliament.) It was not, however, the end of the election, for the other two candidates now demanded that a poll should be held and each party prepared next day to bring up its registered electors. At this point a sensation was caused by the withdrawal of the Tory candidate and the decision of his supporters to give their votes to the 'Cobbettite' candidate, William Turner, who was an ally of the Tories against the middle-class reformers. This manoeuvre proved decisive, for though, on the first day of polling, Bowring and the other liberal candidate were still ahead, Bowring's committee had by then produced virtually all his supporters and Turner was able to bring out enough registered electors to put himself thirteen votes ahead of Bowring.

The defeat of their candidate, whose success had seemed assured, roused Bowring's supporters to fury and allegations of corruption by means of bribery and threats were hurled against his opponents. On the evening after the election an angry crowd gathered outside the Bull Inn where the victors were celebrating their success. There they began attacking the constables and smashing the windows of the inn and would probably have invaded the building itself had not Bowring, who had been hurriedly sent for, arrived on the scene and persuaded them to desist. But, as the *Blackburn Gazette* sorrowfully recorded, 'great excitement continued to prevail during the remainder of the day and also on Friday when some windows were broken at the Wellington and Mitre public houses where the Turner party were drinking'.

Bowring's defeat at Blackburn brought to an end his chances of obtaining a seat in the first reformed parliament, though he tried unsuccessfully to secure his nomination at other places. (At this period not all constituencies held their elections on the same day.) When a vacancy occurred in the City of London early in 1833, Thompson wrote to Place suggesting that Bowring's nomination by the reformers 'would be the heaviest blow in favour of free trade that it would now be possible to strike'. Place, however, who had not forgotten Bowring's reputation in the City at the time of the Greek loan revelations, replied that Bowring's nomination 'would not do'. He gave a similar answer to a letter from Bowring himself, soliciting his help over a vacancy at Preston. It was, in fact, to be two years before a general election in 1835 gave Bowring the opportunity of standing for parliament again and this was to be for the same constituency – Blackburn – where he had been defeated in 1832. He was again to fail there, though, on this occasion, an opportunity in Scotland was at last to gain him admission to the House of Commons.

In addition to Bentham's affairs, his unsuccessful electoral campaign at Blackburn, his work as secretary of the Public Accounts Commission and his commercial investigations in France, a host of other matters demanded Bowring's attention, which he could ill afford, in any sense of the word, to neglect. These included some remaining responsibilities with Thompson's *Westminster Review* and the completion, or abandonment, of various verse translations, including *Songs of Scandinavia*. As Bowring wrote to Thomson from France on one occasion, 'had I now the power of making myself *sept-partiti*, I could find wherewithal to use every sub-division of myself'. All this 'constant vibration', as he described it, was done by a man now approaching middle age. In 1831 Thomas Carlyle, who contributed an article to the *Westminster Review*, gave his wife a vivid description of Bowring at this period of his life. 'Figure to yourself a thin man about my height and bent in the middle into an angle of 150 degrees, the back quite straight, with large, grey eyes, a huge turn up nose . . . and large projecting close cut mouth – figure such a one walking restlessly about the room (for he had been thrown out of a gig and was in pain), fresh of speech, vivid, emphatic and *verstandig*. Such is the radical Doctor'.

Bowring had little opportunity at this period for relaxation with his family at Queen's Square or at Larkbear. In 1830–31, he crossed the channel to Paris no less than five times and visited Brussels more than once. He attended meetings at Paris in company with Parnell or Thomson or later with Villiers and two French commissioners. The investigations of the French Public Accounts went smoothly (as the Orleanist government was seeking the goodwill of Britain) and Bowring was eventually paid for three reports. But the Anglo-French commercial enquiries, which opened in 1832, soon ran into difficulty and Bowring was sent on long tours through the centre and south of France to agitate the silk manufacturers and wine merchants against governmental restrictions on Anglo-French trade. No less than three such tours took place between 1832 and 1834, involving Bowring in long coach journeys from Paris to Lyons, Marseilles, Bordeaux and elsewhere and into Brittany, where he admitted to being 'terribly fracassé by travelling'. Whether Bowring, as a government emissary, was accompanied by any man-servant on his constant travels is unrecorded, nor is there much information about his other activities, which included meetings with leading literary figures, such as the poet Lamartine, as well as with the political refugees from oppressed European peoples, such as the Poles. Although Bowring's official reports to Thomson and long affectionate letters to Villiers (who did not accompany him on these tours) have been preserved, hardly any letters to his wife or other members of his family have come to light for these years.

At first Bowring was full of confidence about the success of the commercial negotiations. 'Engaged in this great work', he wrote to Thomson, 'I often feel that I speak with the tongue of an angel (pardon my vanity) – but I am so perpetually occupied with it that nothing seems like an impediment'. But as frustrations mounted up over the months, Bowring began showing signs of strain, particularly when he ran into opposition at Paris from protectionist ministers. 'What a disgusting business it is to be poking this dunghill about with sharp-pronged pitchforks every day of one's life', he complained to Villiers in June 1833 in sturdy Devonshire brogue; 'since I found the state of things here I am become a boiling cauldron'. His relations with Adolphe Thiers, the Minister of Commerce, were particularly poor. 'I must come to England', he wrote to Villiers from Rouen, 'and we must decide how to crop the ears of the donkies and how to clip the vultures' claws . . . we will concoct a case – propose it to the French government . . . and then let that slippery sagacious scoundrel yclept, Minister of Commerce, bedevil the matter if he can. But he wont – if his nose does not turn up at assafoedita – whose should?' On one occasion Thiers broke into 'an absolute frenzy of abuse', running up and down the room and accusing Bowring of being a charlatan and a theorist who treated him as if he was a child. At another time Bowring forced his way into the presence of Thiers, seized him by the collar and demanded that a tariff amendment allowing the export of raw silk should be immediately put into effect. 'It was a bold stroke, perhaps, to go to a minister and tell him he was a detected rogue', Bowring admitted to Thomson. 'He told me

I was assuming a dictatorial tone and that if such language was used it should be from an ambassador and not from an ambiguous person like me – and this enabled me to say that it was Bowring speaking to Thiers – and not England to France – and that if the ambassador had been here – he would have heard fewer wholesome and useful truths'. The collar incident reached the ears of the Whig government and Villiers was advised to warn Bowring 'to let off some steam but not to work his engine at such very high pressure'.

During these hectic years of 'insurrectionising' the merchants and manufacturers in the French provinces, Bowring somehow managed to get into print the first two volumes of his children's book, *Minor Morals for Young People*. These were published in 1834 and 1835 with illustrations by William Heath and George Cruikshank, who had already produced illustrations for a German children's story translated by Bowring in 1824, *Peter Schlemihl*, 'the Man who lost his Shadow'. The success of this venture may have encouraged Bowring to produce his three volumes of moral stories, particularly as the market for verse translations had declined. He may also have been influenced by the recent success of Harriet Martineau's children's tale, *The Orphan Family*, as well as by the earlier caution-ary tales of Mrs Sherwood and Mrs Trimmer, not to mention Mrs Barbauld's *Hymns in Prose for Children*, on which Bowring himself would have been brought up as a child. *Minor Morals*, 'affectionately dedicated to my wife and children', was a kind of young person's *Deontology*, which Bowring had published from Bentham's papers in the previous year. The first volume, in particular, was well received. That Bowring had assistance with *Minor Morals* seems inevitable in view of his vast number of other commitments. It probably came from Mary Hennell, who was rewarded with a copy of the d'Angers bronze medallion of Bowring's head for her assistance with his writ-ings. The Hennells were Unitarian friends of the Bowring family and Mary's brother, Charles, gave Bowring's eldest son, John, some early commercial experience.

Many of the tales included in *Minor Morals* must have been written in earlier years, as there are frequent references to Bowring's experi-ences in Spain, though a description of a visit to a French prison in 1832 indicates some more recent additions. As stated in the preface to the first volume, the book was intended to illustrate the Utilitarian 'theory of general morals . . . for the service of the young' and reflects

42

Bowring's allegiance to Bentham's 'greatest happiness' principle. Bentham himself, 'the Greatest Philosopher of our days', is mentioned in one of the stories. These provided lessons on courage, generosity, vivacity, justice and other virtues along with 'humanity to animals', 'love of flowers', 'nobility of skin' and, in the second volume, the 'songs of the People'. The mild Mr Howard, whose family were 'always busy in improving and serving one another', bears more resemblance to Bowring's father than to Bowring himself, though he is described as having 'travelled much and studied much' and was 'universally loved'. The somewhat genteel tone of the moral tales themselves, stressing the virtues of prudence and benevolence, raises some interesting considerations. Thus at the very time Mr Howard was urging his young family to avoid 'being angry with any person merely because his opinion was not your opinion' and was illustrating the unpleasant effects of not doing so, Bowring was engaged in a heated correspondence with Chadwick over George Bentham's claims to the possession of his uncle's manuscripts and collaring a French politician for his resistance to tariff reductions. The denunciations of war in the second volume, 'of all plagues the most pestilential, the most prolific', also give pause for reflection. However the benevolent and didactic tone adopted in *Minor Morals* could be used by Bowring when it suited him to do so. He reminded his son, Frederick, in 1839 that 'you have all been trained not in harshness but in love – not with severity to enforce submission and obedience – but in trust and hope of gentleness' and this comes close to the sentiments and style of *Minor Morals*. The three children of *Minor Morals* are never clearly personalized in the tales and it is impossible to identify them with particular members of Bowring's family. The choice of the two boys' names, Arthur and George, which are not those of any Bowring's sons, may have been deliberately made to avoid identification and though his daughter born in 1831 was named Edith, the 'Edith' of *Minor Morals* is probably closer to Maria. The character of 'Marmaduke Method' in one of the tales, to whom 'the value of money was habitually present' and who 'cultivated habits of regularity and order' sounds much like Bowring himself in his early years. (The man portrayed in one of Heath's illustrations also bears a resemblance to Bowring.)

The third and final volume of *Minor Morals* appeared in 1839 but sold less well than its predecessors. It was clearly influenced by

Bowring's tour of Egypt in 1837–8, reflecting, as it did, his enthusiasm for Mehemet Ali. The anecdotes bear a resemblance to the multifarious information about the Near East in his official report on Egypt. Two letters to his children written by Bowring in Paris sound rather like Mr Howard in *Minor Morals*. Lewin and Frederick are congratulated for their successes at school; 'to both of you I say well done, for he does well who does all he can ... When I see good children, as I often do, I like to compare them with you – when bad children, I contrast them'. Maria, now 16, and staying at Exeter, was informed that her father had visited his old prison at Boulogne and that King Louis Philippe had been given a copy of *Minor Morals* for his son. 'I quite expected how you would find Larkbear', her father wrote, 'it was so when I was a boy – it *is* so now my children have the pleasure of enjoying it'.

Bowring's commercial missions to France, and those to Belgium and Switzerland which followed, achieved little success in terms of tariff reductions or trade agreements but they relieved Bowring's financial difficulties. In 1831, when he was still short of funds and was trying to obtain subscribers for his anthology of Bohemian verse, he had confided to his Czech collaborator, Celakovsky, 'I do not care about gain – I was once rich – I am now poor and with seven children I must run no risks'. Four years later, however, he assured Lant Carpenter, 'I am at present under small anxiety as regards my family. I can bear any present sacrifice'.

More important, Bowring's commercial tours introduced him to aristocratic patrons who would further the careers both of Bowring himself and of his sons in the years ahead. George Villiers, who was to become ambassador to Spain and eventually, as Lord Clarendon, Foreign Secretary, remained on cordial terms with Bowring, who wrote to him in most affectionate tones during the French commercial missions 'I am a widowed dove without you'. Villiers did much to assist both Bowring and his sons, though he was not above poking fun at 'the quack Doctor Bow-Wow' with his own aristocratic friends. One of these great ladies, Lady Emily Eden, found the plebeian Bowring an amusing character, declaring that 'barring his detestable manner there is a good deal to like in him. He is so intelligent and quick. And then, with such a fund of vanity that it must be mortified ten times a day. He never lets the mortification call on his temper but is always good humoured and obliging ... They say the first time he dined with Leopold [King of the Belgians], he tripped lightly across the circle of ladies up to the Queen and hanging negligently over her chair, asked her how she liked the thought of leaving her little boy'.

Lord Granville, British ambassador at Paris during Bowring's commercial missions, was another patron who was to help Bowring's son Edgar on various occasions during his years of public employment. Most important of all, the Foreign Secretary, Lord Palmerston, who disliked Bowring's radical opinions, came to think well of his commercial reports and was responsible for several of his later appointments. 'He is a very good humoured lively and agreeable and well informed man', Palmerston wrote to his brother in 1836, 'a complete republican in his opinions . . . However, you should be civil to him. He professes great regard for me and, indeed, I have been useful to him. His commercial reports are able documents and contain much useful information'. In addition, there were old friends of Bowring, such as Edward Ellice (brother-in-law of the first Whig Prime Minister, Lord Grey) and J. C. Hobhouse (Byron's old companion), both of whom had been associated with Bowring since his Greek Committee days and were to assist both Bowring and his sons in securing appointments in government service.

In 1835, three years after his failure to win a seat at Blackburn, Bowring at last secured election to parliament as a member for the reformed constituency of Clyde Burghs (Kilmarnock), joining the small group of philosophical radicals committed to Utilitarian reform. But in 1836, during the recess, he was sent on a commercial mission to the Italian States, on which his eldest son, John, accompanied him. The tour included an interview at Rome with the Pope, who mistook Bowring for an Irish catholic, and with the Grand Duke of Tuscany at Florence. However, the poor state of official records made reliable commercial statistics almost impossible to obtain. After visiting the Austrian provinces of Venice and Trieste, Bowring returned early to England, having contracted an attack of 'marsh fever' (probably malaria), but John remained at Naples in the employment of a British commercial firm.

A year later, after the coronation election of 1837, in which he lost his seat for Clyde Burghs – he had fallen foul of some of his Scottish Presbyterian constituents, as well as of local opponents of Free Trade – Bowring was sent by Palmerston on an important commercial fact-finding mission to Egypt. He was to be abroad for a full year, visiting the Egyptian occupied territories in Syria and Palestine as well as Egypt itself and developing a strong enthusiasm for Pasha Mehemet Ali and his supposed reforms, which were presented as including the abolition of the slave trade.

For nearly five months Bowring remained in Egypt, gathering impressions of the 'vague but civilising purposes of Mehemet Ali' and collecting information which was to be embodied in his report. He visited the villages and noted with approval the attempts of the government to improve agriculture by an ambitious programme of irrigation. He inspected factories for the manufacture of cloth and the distilling of rum, but felt that the workers would be better employed on the land than in handling machines they inadequately understood. He collected such facts as were available upon the extent of disease and pointed out the absurdities of the quarantine regulations. He attempted to inspect the Public Accounts, which were brought to him in huge volumes carried upon the backs of camels. He studied the question of a canal route from the Mediterranean to the Red Sea and gave the opinion that 'serious and detailed investigation should examine the extent of impediments and the means of vanquishing them'. Like most travellers in Egypt, he visited the pyramids and arranged for the despatch of a sphinx to the British Museum, though the sphinx was unfortunately destroyed in a fire at Plymouth dockyard.

Early in 1838 he embarked on a journey up the Nile to the frontiers of Nubia. There he encountered a large body of slaves and felt 'strongly tempted to buy a young girl with no other object than to instruct her and give her freedom'. But he decided that 'the presence of the buyer is the encouragement of the seller' and that the prohibition to purchase, even for the purpose of emancipation, was the wrong course to adopt. He formed the opinion that 'nothing would more tend to abolish the slave trade than the establishment of English agents, and, if possible, of commercial factories at Kartoum, Cordofan and other places in Eastern Africa connected with the Nile'. As he noted in his report, 'the Imaum of Muscat has very lately offered any portion of his territory to the British for the purpose of settlement and expresses a willingness to support an operation for the extinction of the slave trade'. As Bowring enthusiastically wrote to Granville in a letter urging the government to support the *Pasha* at

Cairo rather than the Sultan at Constantinople, 'how important to us is the consolidation of good government of Egypt with a view to its being now and daily becoming more the great highway between the East and the West'.

Once again John accompanied his father and was taken on the journey up the Nile dressed in the uniform of the *Pasha*'s army. To his brother Frederick's amusement, he had the experience of 'drinking coffee with the *Pasha* and smoking his pipe seated on the divan' at his palace in Cairo. While John returned to his office desk at Naples, Bowring continued his tour to Constantinople, where he correctly predicted the inability of the Sultan's forces to withstand the forces of Mehemet Ali's son, Ibrahim Pasha, in a war between the two countries. Returning home via Vienna, where he stayed only briefly, Bowring sent frequent messages to the Foreign Secretary, urging him to support Egyptian independence from Turkish control and emphasising the value to Britain of a steamship route to India via Egypt and the Red Sea rather than the Persian Gulf. When Mehemet Ali threatened to declare his independence in 1838, Bowring was blamed in diplomatic circles for encouraging him to do so. According to Bowring's erstwhile friend, King Louis Philippe, Bowring was the agent at Alexandria of the revolutionary party in Europe, who in every quarter were using their utmost efforts to bring about a war between the Great Powers. 'I mentioned', Granville informed Palmerston, 'that Bowring was a peaceable man though his opinions might be erroneous as to the best means of preserving peace'.

As usual, Bowring's experiences in the Near East were described to family and friends after his return home. He informed an acquaintance in Cornwall, whom he visited in the company of an Egyptian Bey inspecting the industrial resources of the country, that the first verses he heard in the Holy Land were from one of his hymns 'which had been imported and translated by the American missionaries'. The young Caroline Fox, who recorded his visit in her diary, considered Bowring 'a very striking personage with a most poetical, ardent, imaginative forehead and a temperament all in keeping'. In the summer of 1838, still full of enthusiasm for Mehemet Ali and Egypt, Bowring set off for the north, partly to campaign for Free Trade, partly in search of a way back into Parliament, where, as he explained to his Egyptian friends, he could ventilate his views on the Eastern

Question. On 10 September he addressed a meeting of about sixty cotton manufacturers at a hotel in Manchester on the benefits of British commerce to the Near East. The occasion was to be a memorable one because, as a result of a proposal made at the meeting, there was formed the Manchester Anti-Corn Law Association, which was destined to become the nucleus of the Anti-Corn Law League. Bowring's speech at the meeting is also of some interest in view of his recent travels. 'What a satisfaction it is', he declared, 'to every man going from the West to the East, when he clambers up Mount Lebanon to find one of the ancient Druses clothed in garments with which our industrious countrymen provided him. What a delight it is on going to the Holy City to stop with the caravan at Nazareth and scarcely be able to fix upon one to whom your country has not presented some comfort or decoration'. Whatever the truth of Bowring's main assertion about the market for British cotton goods (an assertion he was to reiterate in China), the inference that he had himself been to Jerusalem was misleading as, in fact, an outbreak of plague prevented him from ever visiting the Holy City, though he may have reached Nazareth. He certainly visited the river Jordan, as he filled a bottle of water for the young Queen Victoria.

In the summer of 1839, Palmerston, who had refused, at Granville's insistence, to send Bowring back to France because 'a very strong prejudice will excite against all he says or does', despatched Bowring on a commercial mission to Prussia. On this trip he was accompanied by Lewin, who was being prepared, like his brother John, for a commercial career and had been considered the best German scholar in his Exeter school. Bowring's commercial mission to Prussia, however, achieved little, though it convinced him and other free-traders that the duties on imported corn must be repealed if the efforts of the Zollverein (the Prussian customs union, which covered much of Germany) to keep out British manufacturers were to be frustrated. It was the last occasion on which Bowring was to be employed by the Whig government. Disraeli and other conservatives had been attacking Bowring's employment for several years, pointing out that much of the information collected by Bowring at Berlin and elsewhere could have been obtained more cheaply and in a more up-to-date form from officials on the spot. Moreover, by 1840 relations between the Whigs and the radicals had so far deteriorated that the employment of a free-trade enthusiast as unpredictable as Bowring had become unacceptable to Lord Melbourne and many of his colleagues. 'Damn him', exclaimed Melbourne on one occasion, 'why, he collared a Prime Minister!' The Foreign Office and Board of Trade had discovered other agents, such as Henry Bulwer, who were as useful as Bowring as commercial agents and more discreet in negotiation. Bowring's aggressive and zealous approach had antagonised not only foreign politicians, such as Thiers, but some British officials as well. At Berlin, the British minister praised Bowring's zeal and discretion as a negotiator, but a few years earlier the ambassador at Brussels, Sir Robert Adair, had complained to Palmerston about derogatory comments made by Bowring at a banquet which he took to refer to himself. ('Heigh-Ho!' wrote Bowring to Villiers about this incident, 'would that the cholera might sweep the old diplomatic cobwebs away . . .'.) Former supporters of Bowring, like Thomson, with whom Bowring had quarrelled over the reports on his French commercial missions, had either left the government or become antagonistic to him over his enthusiasm for Mehemet Ali. Palmerston, in particular, considerably cooled towards him, though the rift was healed after the Foreign Secretary's diplomatic success in 1840–41 in securing Egyptian withdrawal from Syria, following British naval bombardment of the coast of the Levant. It was an event which aroused Bowring's strong indignation – 'We are to have war and we owe it to the Whigs' – but it bore a striking resemblance to his own action at Canton sixteen years later.

As the chances of being employed on further commercial missions faded, Bowring began making serious efforts to get back into parliament. His experiences illustrated the difficulty for candidates without private means of doing so. In December 1839 his family links with the West Country prompted him to put himself forward for the borough of Penryn and Falmouth, one of the most corrupt constituencies in the country, where a vacancy had occurred. A more unsuitable seat for a person of Bowring's limited financial means could scarcely have been found, for it was common knowledge that the first rich man of either party who was prepared to spend £3000 on the election would win. Addressing the electors at Penryn, he found the audience completely indifferent to his opinions, though they kept 'slapping their pockets, thereby signifying . . . it was to that region and not to their reason or conscience that his arguments should be addressed'. According to one account, 'the only thing in his speech that at all touched them was his declaration that he was half a Cornishman, his mother being the daughter of the clergyman and schoolmaster of St Ives, Mr Lane, whose memory is still held in the odour of sanctity'. After a similar experience at Falmouth, Bowring decided that his position was hopeless and he withdrew from the contest.

During the next year or so Bowring made regular efforts to find a constituency where he could rely on enthusiasm for Free Trade and radical support rather than corrupt electors. An invitation to stand as official candidate for the Anti-Corn Law League at Walsall was dropped in face of local resentment and though he stood at Kirkaldy Burghs in a by-election, he came bottom of the poll. In May 1841 he considered a joint candidature with Colonel Thompson at Hull and even thought of standing again at Blackburn. In June, however, he received, on Richard Cobden's recommendation, an offer from the Lancashire textile city of Bolton and was formally adopted by the liberals as a Free Trade candidate at the forthcoming general election. This took place at Bolton in the presence of a great crowd of working people from the mills. When the poll was taken both liberal candidates were elected by a large majority, Bowring, whose campaign had cost him little, was delighted with the result, assuring the electors that in parliament he would 'legislate for the benefit of all'. The local Tory newspaper, however, described him as 'a confessed cast-off with a name little to be coveted ... He is a quack, a pragmatical and dangerous man'. (As usual the 'Greek Pie' was mentioned during the election.) But although the Tories had failed to win at Bolton, where Free Trade sentiment was strong, in the country as a whole the verdict was different. When Bowring took his seat in the new parliament in August 1841, the Whig government was defeated and Peel accepted office as leader of a five-year Conservative administration.

4

The Member of Parliament for Bolton

When Bowring returned to parliament as MP for Bolton in 1841, the older offspring in his family were taking their first steps towards independence and, with their father's help, the making of a career for themselves. After his return from Germany, Lewin was granted by Hobhouse, who was President of the Board of Control, a writership in the Indian Civil Service to be preceded by a period of training at the East India College at Haileybury. 'I hope for a quiet talk with Hobhouse about Lewin', Bowring wrote to his wife from Exeter in 1840, 'perhaps to obtain him some advantages for the future'. Lewin in fact, did very well at Haileybury and in due course was to sail for Bengal. In 1841, however, Bowring, back in Parliament, launched at attack on the East India Company for its alleged ill-treatment of a deposed *rajah*. Hobhouse, now out of office, was furious and wrote to Ellice; 'as you were the person at whose solicitation I gave his son a writership, perhaps you will . . . ask him to put off his Motion for a reasonable day, when I can attend and make my defence . . . In this case, I really believe money is given and received – nothing else can account for such preposterous conduct. I would write to Bowring myself, but I do not think it safe to trust pen to paper with him'. Ellice tried to calm Hobhouse down, agreeing that Bowring had acted like a fool, and Hobhouse's anger eventually subsided. But it was one of several examples of Bowring as MP alienating former friends by allowing his reforming zeal to overcome his tact. The Unitarian minister, Joseph Hunter (an old friend of Bowring's brother-in-law, Thomas Ward), had been much put out by Bowring's overbearing treatment of him before a Select Committee in 1836.

By the time Lewin secured his appointment to the East India

'Living Litterateurs' – Dr Bowring *Pictorial Times*, June 1844

Company, Frederick was attending Trinity College, Cambridge, the college, according to his father, 'where there are perhaps most temptations'. Bowring, who had hesitated to send his son to an Anglican university, was full of solicitude about his welfare. 'I rely on you with such thorough confidence', he wrote, 'that I shall not hesitate to trust you among all temptations that you will do right. You know that I am stretching a point for your benefit and I look to your good conduct as my ample reward' (January 1840). When Frederick confessed to 'feelings of anxiety and loneliness', his father assured him 'all will go well with you while carrying out your resolution of diligence and virtue'. He urged Frederick (who needed no urging in this respect) to take 'a daily walk ... eight hours a day of devotion to study is enough. As you make intelligent acquaintances your studies will be relieved and assisted by conversation' (27 October 1840). Frederick, who years later described his first year at Trinity as the happiest time of his life, soon settled down, obtained a good degree in the mathematics tripos (though he declared himself 'thoroughly disgusted' with his result) and was granted a five-year fellowship at Trinity, where his youngest brother, Charles, eventually joined him.

In these years Edgar, who had first attended 'Mr Chennell's School' in Mare Street, Hackney, was a pupil at the London University School (in a wing of the college), run on Utilitarian lines and well ahead in *curriculum* and disciplinary methods of most of its contemporaries. Here his youngest brother, Charles, was eventually to join him before proceeding, like Frederick, to Trinity College, Cambridge. Bowring was also, at this period, attending to the education of his eldest daughter. Little is known about the early years of his daughters or about their education, which in Maria's case must have been a broken one. In 1839 Maria was sent to Paris for some months to perfect herself in French. 'Sister is very much improved and we are quite delighted with her', wrote Frederick to his mother from Exeter after her return. 'She sings very nicely and that is an amusement of an evening to us, for we have not heard her play on the piano for three years and she has wonderfully improved in that time'. Genteel attainments were also pursued by Maria's sisters. Edith perfected herself in German: 'it is considered a lady-like accomplishment nowadays', wrote Frederick, 'in modern languages ladies make just as good scholars as men do'. Emily, too, was later to receive an education at 'the school' – presumably a finishing school – at Exeter, when she was 16 and her father was in China.

'I never saw a family, with such development of intellect,' wrote Mary Hennell in 1841, 'Frederick is first man of his year at Trinity, Cambridge ... Edgar has carried off three prizes at the London University and lots of testimonials. John has an appointment under the first house in the China trade to go out in January and he himself [Bowring] is to take part in the grand free trade fight that is to come.' Everything at last appeared to be going well for Bowring and his family. In August 1841, however, 'a terrible blow was ... to fall on the family in the loss of their little Gertrude', wrote Mary Hennell. 'I called on Mrs B. on Saturday and found the Doctor too; poor Doctor, sadly cut up. I never saw a man so completely oppressed with grief. She bears it much better than he. It was so sudden and the child was the delight of them all, had never been ill, had never given any anxiety. He doted on her and she was an extraordinary little thing; their youngest and brightest, on whom all their hopes for

53

the future were concentrated. Mrs B. bears it like herself, magnani-
mously as she does all great things far better than the Doctor – he
looked admiringly at her as he said so to me. I am going again this
morning. He thanked me for coming though he could hardly speak
correctly and said his head felt quite confused. It seemed so cruel,
just when he was all alive, entering on his fresh political career.
Edgar has got a place at the Board of Trade, £80 p.a. to increase to
£500 in three years'.

Gertrude's death of scarlet fever was the first of several family
shocks Bowring and his wife were now to experience. His two unmarried sisters had already deserted George's Meeting and become regular attendants at Exeter Cathedral. Then, early in 1843, two years
after her brothers and sisters had all been baptised by a Unitarian
minister at Exeter (as a family Bible testifies), Maria became a
member of the established church. Soon after came a letter from
Frederick addressed to his 'dear parents':

> Loth as I was to give either of you pain, I thought it better to
> apply to you at once than delay any longer. I was baptised by
> Mr Slatter, a lay-vicar at the cathedral. He is I believe, the one
> who baptised Maria and he promised himself the pleasure of
> calling at Queen's Square next week as he is going to stay near
> London for a week or two. He is the composer of some of the
> anthems used in this cathedral and a very good musician. Hope
> Mamma has recovered from her illness. (25 June 1843)

The change of Frederick to Anglicanism is understandable, for as a
non-conformist he would have been unable to take a Cambridge
degree, much less hold a fellowship. The decision, however, gave his
father 'some pain':

> But far less pain than I should feel if I could believe for a
> moment that you would conceal your wishes or purposes from
> one who loves you as I love you and desires your happiness . . .
> nor could I dream of denying to my children the right and duty
> of that private judgment which I have always struggled to obtain
> for everybody . . . I shall not trouble you with controversy about
> the merits or demerits of the Church you join. I hope you will
> always remember that the best and truest part of any religion

must be candour and charity to others ... the creed of intolerance is alike worthless and wicked. (25 June 1843)

Frederick was to remain an inveterate Low-Churchman throughout his life, holding views which made it difficult for him to reconcile himself to more extensive religious changes by other members of his family.

In spite of his many parliamentary and business activities the future of his sons remained Bowring's pre-eminent concern. In 1842, after the Treaty of Nanking had opened several Chinese ports, in addition to Canton, to British trade, his eldest son John, back from his commercial experience in Italy, went out to China in the employment of Jardine Matheson and Co., the most powerful British merchants in the South China seas and soon destined to play a leading role in Hong Kong after its cession to the British Crown. The circumstances of John's appointment by Jardine Matheson are obscure but may have been due to his father's friendship with John Abel Smith, chief partner in Smith, Payne and Smith, Bowring's bankers in England. Both John Smith and his father had contributed to the confidential fund raised by his friends to assist Bowring out of his financial difficulties in 1828. Smith, who was a liberal Member of Parliament, seems to have assisted Jardine Matheson in bringing pressure on the Whig government to act resolutely at Canton. Bowring, who in his days as radical MP opposed the opium trade, always acted circumspectly in his dealing with Jardine Matheson and Co., who were among the biggest opium dealers in the Far East.

A year after John went to China, Lewin, who had carried off several prizes at Haileybury, including 'two handsome volumes' for Sanskrit and Arabic, set sail for India bearing a letter of introduction from Lord Clarendon (formerly George Villiers) to the Governor-General, Lord Ellenborough. 'Lewin says that if his grandpapa and aunts were to come to London', Bowring wrote to his wife, 'it would only lead to a scene at his departure which he had rather avoid – and on the whole I think he is right. You and me he can trust for a little more self-possession but even as it is I tremble for the moment when we must break away. The lad is my father's pride and joy and they will never meet again – at least it is little likely they should. But this is a subject on which it is painful – far too painful to dwell' (22 September 1843). (Lewin later wrote on the letter, 'I returned in

October 1854, my grandfather had till April 1856 but was waning fast when I saw him again'.)

In 1844 Frederick decided to embark on a course of legal training with an eye to becoming a barrister after the termination of his five-year Cambridge fellowship. His father urged him to study Bentham 'my venerable master . . . I shall not ask you to adopt his principles – but to weigh his reasonings'. Edgar, meanwhile, entered the Board of Trade in 1841, where he was remain for over 20 years, his appointment owed mainly to Lord Clarendon, now a rising figure in the Whig party. There remained Bowring's youngest son, Charles, who had followed Edgar to the London University School and was making 'excellent progress in languages'. But Charles was already giving indications of the problems which lay ahead. As his father wrote to Frederick:

He has in him a strange mingling of attention and indifference, present knowledge – absent habits. He forgets nothing and everything. His head is always busy yet might fall off his shoulders without his knowing it. Happily for him it is fastened on – for hats, gloves, garments which are not fastened on – depart from him day by day. (22 August 1842)

Bowring already had thoughts of sending him to China or India in the wake of his two elder brothers. 'I am constantly turning over in my mind plans for his coming destiny', he wrote, 'should I not succeed in getting a writership for him. He certainly looks towards the East and I think John's and Lewin's expectations win his fancies towards the rising sun' (17 October 1842).

The return of Bowring to Parliament in 1841 enabled him to resume the role his 'master', Bentham, had planned for him as expositor of his theories in the House of Commons. As during his former membership, his votes and fairly frequent, though brief, speeches reflect the reformist causes with which as a philosophical radical and free-trader he was concerned. As he had written, somewhat self-importantly, to Carpenter after his first election to Parliament in 1835, 'I feel it my duty to do what depends on me for giving a liberal direction to our foreign and domestic policy with whose liberalism I am to a certain degree (and perhaps more than is generally known) associated . . . and there to assist that inevitable and (as

56

I thought) speedy triumph of the good and generous principle – of whose triumph I doubted never and less than ever now'. The matters on which he spoke and voted during nearly seven years as a MP read like a catalogue of his declared political aims. At the top of the list was the abolition of the corn duties and the reduction of other tariffs. As one of the sitting members, he pressed for the relief of distress in Bolton and for a more humane application of his former ally Chadwick's system of poor relief. As a supporter of *laissez-faire*, however, he was opposed to the regulation of wages, a point of view which, in spite of assurances that he had their interests at heart, had lost him the support of the handloom weavers during his previous membership of parliament. He advocated a further measure of parliamentary reform and the ballot and, less ostentatiously, the other Chartist six points. He favoured the extension of popular education with rate-supported local schools. The list of his parliamentary priorities included the revision of the quarantine regulations (a subject on which Bowring felt strongly in view of his experiences in the Near East and elsewhere), the abolition of flogging in the army (which took place at the barracks near his home in Queen's Square, Westminster), the reform of the Colonial Accounts and the implementations of long-delayed changes advocated by the Public Accounts Committee, of which he had been secretary. He advocated the introduction of decimal coinage, later producing a book on this subject and claiming to be the originator of the two shilling piece, the florin. He supported the suppression of the opium trade (though his situation on this matter was already a delicate one) and the worldwide abolition of slavery. (His appearance as delegate for Exeter at an anti-slavery convention in 1840 is recorded in a painting at the National Portrait Gallery.) He achieved a small success with the reduction of the customs duties in the Isle of Man and in 1844 both he and his wife were given a rousing reception at Douglas. A street on the island was even named after him. He tried to secure similar reductions for Malta, from which he received a silver salver on his way to China. He championed the claims of foreign exiles, mainly from Italy and Poland, criticising the opening of the mail of political refugees by the Post Office. He became chairman of the People's International League, instigated in 1847 by Mazzini. The secretary of the League, the journalist W. J. Linton, thought 'there

57

was a little of the Girondist, of the pedagogue' about Bowring, 'but he was a good citizen and a man to be respected'.

In 1844 a pen portrait of Bowring as MP, 'in that plebeian carriage called a 'bus', was published in the *Pictorial Times*, together with an engraving of Bowring seated beside a bust of Bentham:

He had a parliamentary report and an old *Quarterly Review* under one arm, a new number of the *Westminster Review* in one hand and a damp double *Times* newspaper with a supplement in the other ... a shabby hat adorned his head, a pair of steel spectacles his nose, and his whole upper person was adorned in black and in black of some standing ... He sat in a perfect fidget, attempted to open the *Times* but failed, unsuccessfully fumbled the whole of his pockets through for a penknife and then buried spectacles and all in the half opened pages of the *Westminster Review* ... He called the conductor to stop and left the omnibus in a state of curious solicitude and perplexity ... Burke looked a great man standing under an archway to escape a shower; Dr. Bowring will be glad to know that he looked a great man even in an omnibus.

Two years earlier, the *Illustrated London News* had published a 'Popular Portrait', in which Bowring was described as 'one of the reform philosophers of the age, a gentleman who has given his life to languages and liberalism; a traveller; a commercialist; a Benthamite and a Member of Parliament of considerable public usefulness and of no small repute'. 'Dr Bowring is one of the free doctrine group of legislators of the Grote and Thompson school', explained the *News*, 'and a pet of the Whigs during their administration ... He received the ordinary education of the middle classes of society and was taught the elements of the classics and mathematics at a country school near Dartmoor whose wild and romantic scenery made on his young mind a stronger impression than the lessons of the dissenting teacher'. After emphasising his precocity as a linguist, the writer gave a list of no less than 32 'modern continental languages' and dialects of which Bowring was said to have acquired 'an easy command'. This spectacular catalogue was followed by a description of the honours he had received from European sovereigns, including a diamond ring from the Emperor of Russia and a gold medal with a laudatory inscription from the King of Holland, 'and he was made a knight of the Order of Christ by the Queen of Portugal'.

During his years in Parliament a more substantial product of Bowring's 'unceasing literary labours' (as the *News* described them) appeared in *The Collected Works of Jeremy Bentham*, published in 1843 in eleven volumes. The laborious task of arranging Bentham's writings, many in manuscript form, had been carried out by various admirers of the philosopher, as Bowring himself was constantly abroad or involved in other duties. These included Dr Southwood Smith, who had performed the dissection on Bentham's body and who acted as Bowring's representative with the Edinburgh publisher, William Tait; the Edinburgh journalist, J. Hill Burton, who wrote the general introduction to the *Works*; and Bentham's former secretary, Richard Doane. Other persons connected with the publication of the *Works* included Mary Hennell, who assisted Bowring with the two-volume memoir of Bentham, and members of Bowring's own family. Frederick, for example, copied for his father part of the account of Bentham's life 'which I like very much, though I think there are few who would not wonder at such an extraordinary talent as he possessed at an age when most boys are just beginning Latin'. 'To have known him must have been a great pleasure', Frederick wrote to his mother; 'as I have heard you say that you were one of his most intimate friends, I daresay you can recollect many interesting traits of his character'. It was Bowring himself, however, who decided which works to withhold altogether from the edition, including the *Auto-Icon* and most of his writings on religion, and which extracts from his correspondence to exclude, especially about his own relations with Bentham. *The Collected Works*, which reflected the piecemeal method in which the project was carried out, was severely criticised by the *Edinburgh Review* and has usually received hostile comment since then, (Leslie Stephen considered Bowring's memoir of Bentham one of the worst biographies in the language.) As in Bowring's own *Autobiographical Recollections*, there are certainly more anecdotes in the memoir than there is serious consideration of Bentham's philosophical ideas. But the 1843 *Collected Works* even in its imperfect state did not merit the harsh treatment it received, particularly from opponents of Utilitarianism and enemies of Bowring.

His parliamentary duties made it more difficult for Bowring to find employment abroad after 1841, especially during a conservative administration. He was obliged, therefore, to select fresh means of income to support his family and in 1843 turned once more to commerce, investing his capital in a Welsh industrial concern, the Cambrian Iron and Spelter Works, which he renamed the Llynvi Iron works, forming a partnership with his younger brother, Charles, who became business manager of the new concern. Charles had had a somewhat chequered career working in the family serge business at Exeter and then, like his elder brother, becoming a dealer in sherry wines (Bowring himself tried to secure customers for him). Bowring also began to undertake 'some other weighty concerns in the City', speculating heavily in railway shares and planning a railway in the neighbourhood of his ironworks – the Llynvi Valley Railway. In 1845 he became chairman of the Directors of the London and Blackwall Railway, a short route running from the City to the St Katharine docks. As a frequent traveller, he had been interested in railway development since its earliest days, taking part in 1836 in an abortive project 'for uniting the capitals of France, England and Belgium by railway'. In a letter to Frederick in 1841 he commented on the rapid progress of the Great Western route. 'It will be a comfortable thing to get from London to Larkbear in eight hours, as we shall be able to do by and by', he wrote. (The traditional coach journey took 24 hours or longer by ship). As in the 1820s Bowring soon began to speculate heavily, especially after the revival of trade in 1842. 'Dr Bowring', wrote the author of *The Physiology of London Business* in 1845, 'with his sharp features, puny voice and disquisitions on what Parliament intends to do with railways, has worked himself onto the Blackwall Board there to devise and legislate schemes for its future success . . . He has always something to say, either in shape of suggestions or correction, and is regarded as a whale among minnows . . . Dr Bowring disports his figure at several other Joint Stock Company meetings. He may be seen at the Commercial and one or two of the Australian Banks when dividends are declared'.

By 1844 the 'railway mania' was at its height and the Llynvi Ironworks was doing well. 'You will be glad to hear how prosperously things are going on at Bowrington', Bowring assured Frederick, 'where money is making fast and the iron is becoming silver and gold' (14 February 1845). 'We are most anxious to have four furnaces in blast', he wrote in a later letter after Frederick had visited

Bowrington, 'the demand for iron being very vigorous now. We have been selling largely' (15 September 1845). When a Government commissioner visited Bowrington in 1845, he was impressed by 'the enlightened interest' the Llynvi Iron Company was showing 'in the well being of the working people'. The confidence of Bowring in the mid-1840s was reflected in his public speeches. Free Trade, international co-operation and world peace were his favourite themes. At Anti-Corn Law rallies, industrial congresses and Peace Society conferences, he preached the gospel of enlightened self-interest with the missionary zeal of an apostle. 'Every vessel', he proclaimed, in an address on 'the Political and Commercial Import-ance of Peace', at the Hall of Commerce in London, 'that quits our shores in the pursuit of honest and honourable trade, is a missionary of good, every article of manufacture which by its cheapness or excellence recommends itself to the approval of a purchaser, conveys a moral lesson'. 'We live in a wondrous age', Bowring assured his hearers at the opening of a steam press in 1846. 'Men are beginning to comprehend their interests, to cast away their prejudices, to under-stand each other better than before. National hatred is beginning to disperse itself before love and these changes in the views and feelings of men are leading the way to great and beneficient changes in the commercial and political world ... peace has come among us with all its blessings – we have covered the whole world with means of communication and made advances in the arts and conveniences and ornaments of life greater than in the ten preceding generations. England, instead of being the threatener of the peace of the world, is in the position to offer it a great and glorious example of all that is good and great'.

Behind this high-sounding rhetoric, however, with its suggestion of a rousing speaker, Bowring was becoming increasingly aware of his own political limitations. In spite of the plaudits of the liberal press, his failure to make a favourable impression in the House of Commons had become apparent, even to himself. We are told he had only to get to his feet for many MPs to leave the Chamber. Descriptions of his lack of success as a speaker, which were first heard during his brief tenure as a member for Clyde Burghs in 1835–7, were often made by political opponents and should be taken guardedly. But they are too frequent to be dismissed, coming also from well-wishers. Although the diarist, Crabb Robinson – no uncritical acquaintance of Bowring – thought him much improved after his election in 1835, 'being blessed with assurance, miscellaneous and general knowledge, great facility of speech and a knowledge of modern languages', this was not the general impression. As early as 1836 a sympathetic observer, who considered Bowring 'one of the most useful members' and 'an unrivalled polyglot', was disappointed with his performance in parliament. 'His voice is clear and capable with proper management of being made pleasant to the ear. But he seems to have no control over it'. He also criticized him for 'speaking too often on topics of trifling importance' and for 'never having brought forward a motion on any question of commanding interest'. A comment after Bowring's death about his 'didactic and professorial manner' is reinforced by an 1847 survey of *Orators of the Age*, in which he is described as 'speaking like an aged pedagogue trying to awe a very naughty boy'. He presented his facts 'in a confused jumble without order or arrangement in intricate and imperfect sentences and without anything like a connected chain of thinking'. On one occasion, when he tried to show off his knowledge of Spanish wines and the Spanish language in a speech, he was almost laughed out of the House. All this criticism does not tally easily with other impressions of Bowring as a public speaker. In 1832, after riots broke out following his narrow defeat at Blackburn, he addressed the crowd, according to a liberal newspaper, 'in a most impressive and affectionate manner'. The reports of his addresses at Free Trade meetings give a similar impression, though such reports remain suspect as coming from political supporters. As a speaker at Unitarian functions he was apparently much in demand, as 'he excelled in various styles of oratory, his lectures always delighting numerous audiences'. In private conversation, his volubility was well known. Bentham himself recommended Bowring to the electors of Blackburn for his 'fluency of speech'. John Neal, the American visitor who resided for a time with Bentham, thought Bowring 'a good deal of a chatterbox', but was fascinated at first by his fluency. Sir Walter Scott commented on his 'flux of conversation'. MacFarlane's impressions of his volubility have already been described and Borrow also portrayed him as trying to dominate any conversation. The members of his family are understandably reticent about the matter. Bowring's fluency and fecundity as a letter writer and versifier needs no illustration, though it is worth noting his habit of sprinkling his writing 'with the black pepper of common Latin phrases', as if to put himself on a par with university educated contemporaries brought up in the classical tradition.

In November 1846, after Peel's repeal of the corn duties and the return of the Whigs to office following the split in the Tory party, Bowring wrote a long letter to Ellice, expressing his bitter sense of failure. The letter – one of the most self-revealing Bowring wrote to someone outside the family – is worth quoting in detail:

You have been in all circumstances a kind and useful friend, one to whom I have never hesitated to address myself unreservedly – and I am about to use that privilege now in the persuasion you will understand and appreciate my motives. In the present state of parties I feel it encumbent upon me to look around and to ascertain my own position and prospects. But I will at once relieve you from supposing that I am compelled to ask for any favour from official men. I am happily placed in circumstances of absolute personal independence. I have an income amply adequate to my moderate wants and I have the extreme good fortune to see my five boys – every one of them – crowned with university and other honours – launched with prospects – bright prospects – upon the ocean of life. And moreover though I have been so many years a political partisan, I am not aware that I have ever solicited a personal favour from the government. Even the ordinary patronage, which I suppose may be had for the asking, I have always refused to apply for. I have fought five contested elections – in the last I received Bolton from the hands of a Tory – and I never received a farthing of party money. When, nearly 20 years ago, commercial disasters left me pennyless (I do not forget – I cannot forget – the kindness you and some few friends exhibited then), I was enabled to provide by literary exertions – all in the field of liberal politics – for myself and family. The *Westminster Review*, of which I was then and for many years the Editor, rendered some valuable services to the popular cause. Of the leading writers connected with it almost all are at this moment occupying places of important public trust. In my whole career only one permanent appointment was every offered me – this was in the making up of the Althorp Administration. It was the Consulship of Panama ... In the field of commercial reform you know the part I played in the early negotiations with France. Their results appeared unimportant, yet the trade with that country in consequence of the few changes we were able to obtain has more than trebled. I believe you know too that I wrote the elaborate Reports presented to Parliament on this subject. The two French Commissioners have since become – one the Minister of the Interior – the other a Peer of France. My colleague Lord Clarendon is – and most worthily – the President of the Board of Trade. I – am nothing and nobody.

As to my journeys and long reports on our commercial relations with Germany and Italy and Switzerland and the Levant, they speak for themselves – and form a huge file of contributions to the cause of Free Trade. That cause, too, I have otherwise served – I dare say you do not know – but it is a fact that I was the founder and the baptiser of the Anti-Corn Law League. Its first nucleus originated at a banquet given to me at Manchester and though I have naturally and willingly surrendered my very prominent place to men worthier than myself, I have not been altogether inactive. I wrote the Report of the Import Duties Committee. Next to the League that Report has been deemed one of the most important contributions to the Free Trade movement. At all events it has been translated into every European language and has been a landmark in our Free Trade legislation. I have rendered too some other services both gratuitous and laborious to the public . . . but you will naturally ask why – if I have nothing to ask – why I trouble you? The fact is I do not know how to answer the enquiries which assault me on every side – 'How is it you of all men have been so utterly neglected and thrown aside?' An Election – perhaps an expensive one – cannot be far distant. And it now becomes me seriously to consider whether to break away from public life altogether – or still keep my Parliamentary position – or look in one of the departments to which my attention has been specially directed – that of Public Accounts (which deserves and demands the serious attention of the Government) or the Board of Trade (where I have reason to think an appropriate opening may before long present itself) – for some fixed position of usefulness. Though, as I have said, I am comfortably independent

64

– and able and determined to hold my seat independently (if I shall continue in the House of Commons) I am not without the desire and the ambition to be enabled officially to aid reforms with which my public history has been associated and which are important to the public weal. Do not, my dear Sir, think I fail to appreciate two special acts of kindness – one of which I owe particularly to you and Sir John Hobhouse and the other to Lord Clarendon in connection with my sons. These I gratefully own are most important favours and they weigh heavily against any claims I may be supposed to have. I cheerfully transfer them from that personal kindness in which they originated for their full share to the political account.

Ellice passed on Bowring's letter to the Prime Minister, Lord John Russell – no particular friend of Bowring's, though he had earlier employed him, as a non-conformist, to inspect the Extra-Parochial Registers – with some sympathetic observations:

With all his vanity and some other drawbacks from his useful qualities which I will not insist upon, he has been an industrious labourer in the vineyard, with more merit, if shared with some demerit than many who have acquired more fruit from it and it would be a kindness to send for him, to acknowledge his claims in the cause of reform and to say, as the case may be, whether your limited means of patronage enable you to hold out any likelihood in future of employing him. He has rather won me to his side by the creditable manner in which he has educated his boys. The one, for which Hobhouse gave a writership, gained many prizes both at Haileybury and Calcutta and Hardinge says he is the most promising young man in their service.

There is no evidence, however, that Ellice's letter brought Bowring any immediate prospects of public employment, though it perhaps contributed something to the willingness of the Whig leadership to accept his appointment to Canton two years later.

In the General Election of 1847, Bowring retained his Bolton seat, though with a much reduced majority. But his re-election was soon followed by commercial depression and the collapse of his business concerns. Adverse comments about the London and Blackwall Railway directors had appeared in the press for some time and these were followed by a general drop in the value of railway shares. The Llynvi Valley Railway announced a suspension of all works early in 1848. In November 1847 an extraordinary meeting of the directors of the Llynvi Iron Company had taken place at their London office in Moorgate, at which there was a declaration of a loss on the year's accounts. This was followed by a 10% reduction of wages, which in turn led to a strike and by December the forges were at a standstill. To add to his troubles, in November 1847 Bowring and his brother were robbed by two armed Irishmen on their way to the ironworks with the wages. Though the money was later recovered, the incident caused considerable alarm to Bowring's family and there were reports in the *Times* and mention of it in the House of Commons. Few of Bowring's letters for this period have come to light and there is a gap in his correspondence with Frederick, but it is clear that Bowring was in a worse financial position than at any time since 1828 and was obliged to borrow money from his sons and from various friends. In spite of improvements in other industries, the position in the iron trade continued grave. In June 1848 a Welsh newspaper reported that the export consumption of iron was at the lowest possible ebb. 'Gloomy day', wrote Frederick in a diary he was keeping, of which only fragments survive, 'as gloomy as our prospects. Had a long talk with my mother about our affairs which are making my father wretched. His liabilities appear to thicken around him and I early see we shall all have to bear a good deal of trouble. For my part I think my best plan would be to return to Cambridge for a couple of years, endeavour to make a little money by pupils and read law. At any rate my Fellowship will support Charles' (4 February 1848).

In October 1848, therefore, when Palmerston offered Bowring the vacant consulship at Canton, at a salary of £1800 a year, he accepted it, in spite of his age, with alacrity. The news of the offer arrived in a letter from Clarendon. 'My dear Bowring', he wrote, 'I could not see Palmerston yesterday but have done so today – nobody could be more kind about you than he was, *l'affaire est faite* – the Canton Consulship is yours ... if I do not see you again, Goodbye and God bless you'. Ever since his son John had gone to China in 1842, Bowring had been interested in Chinese affairs. He had been a member of a parliamentary committee on China and had spoken on

Hong Kong in the House of Commons. 'You may suppose my head is somewhat giddy and my heart troubled', he wrote to Frederick, 'but my anxieties about the futurity of you all will be wholly removed'. Meanwhile the uncertainty of his business affairs continued. 'In the gloom which now surrounds us all', he wrote to his son, 'I feel very uncertain whether or not anything will be saved out of the wrecks around. I am quite assured that you will be able in the course of a few years to repay all you have received from me'. On 16 December a short paragraph in the *Times* announced Bowring's appointment to Canton: 'The Learned Gentleman has long been in a state of health which required his residence in a warmer climate. We believe that Sir Joshua Walmsley will succeed Dr Bowring in the representation of Bolton'. Bowring, who declared himself 'too poorly to go to Bolton in person', despatched to his constituency his farewell address, much to the disgust of the Tory *Bolton Chronicle*, which considered that 'to most people the appointment under such conditions will appear monstrous . . . A man of more miserably defective judgement or more thoroughly indiscreet could not have been selected out of the whole range of public men'.

Prior to his departure to China, there was much for Bowring to arrange. This included the sorting out of the material and financial problems at Bowrington, which his brother Charles would have to deal with, the ordering of his investments and other business affairs, which Frederick and Edgar were to manage, the disposal of the house at Queen's Square, Westminster, and the sale of unwanted books and furniture. Above all, there was the move of Bowring's wife and three daughters, who were not accompanying him to China, to the parental home at Exeter, on the grounds that Bowring could not afford two establishments, especially as his aged father and two sisters were partly dependent on his restricted resources.

Even at this eleventh hour, however, another shock lay in store for Bowring. In 1846 his youngest son, Charles, had won a scholarship to Trinity College, his older brothers contributing to the payment of his expenses. His father had become increasingly concerned about his future. As he had written to Frederick (25 April 1848):

I think he would be more happily *niched* at Cambridge than anywhere else. I doubt if in any of the professions the ambitious impulse would be strong enough to impel him forward. He would prefer the seclusion of the study to its application in the busy field of professional competition. He cares nothing about money even as a means of usefulness and advancement. He would be as happy with £500 as with £5000 a year – perhaps happier. I doubt his fitness for the hot rivalry of the fight when many are pressing so eagerly on – but in his library – with all appliances and means of progress – he would get a reputation for learning – and deserve that reputation – which would infallibly lead to his promotion.

Now, at the very moment of Bowring's departure for China, Charles informed his father that he had become a Roman Catholic. In his letters and speeches Bowring had always upheld Catholic toleration. An enthusiastic supporter of the 1829 Emancipation Act – he had been a member of a Unitarian committee with Aspland and Fox, pressing for its adoption – he had voted for the Maynooth Grant in 1845 and as recently as February 1848 had praised the 'reforming Pope', Pius IX, in the House of Commons. Although Bowring had been critical of Jesuit activities in Spain, Frederick was probably correct when he wrote that his father 'preferred the Church of Rome to the Church of England but that is almost certainly a political feeling'. Now in the final letter (16 January 1849) sent to Frederick at Cambridge before leaving England Bowring could not conceal his bitterness:

It is idle to dwell upon shattered and shipwrecked hopes but we must think of what can be done for the dear fellow whose conscience is leading him to such powerful sacrifices and to such grief and gloom. He will probably open his heart to you on the receipt of the note I sent him. Deal tenderly with him – respect his convictions – persuade him quietly to resume his studies – and let us wait to consider how the case is to be dealt with. The shock comes at a terrible moment. I thought the cup of bitterness was filled – but another bitter drop has fallen into it. And to you my beloved Fritz – I give it in special charge not to wound our Charles by animadversions. It is a case for sympathy – for kindness – for anxiety – for distress – but not for blame. So view it – so deal with it.

In January 1849, soon after writing this letter, Bowring left England for China. He was not to see his wife and most of his family again for four and a half years.

5

Her Britannic Majesty's Consul at Canton

The lonely years at Canton provide the most detailed picture of Bowring's family. We have not only his own prolific and homesick correspondence with his sons Frederick and Edgar, much of it about events at home as well as the situation in China, but also many of Frederick's monthly letters to his father at Canton and to his mother at Exeter, as well as a few letters from Bowring's wife to Frederick at Cambridge. These were years fraught with family problems, which their father was ill equipped by distance and circumstance to deal with.

Bowring's 'exile' in China was accepted without bitterness by his family, which saw the Canton consulship as the solution to his overwhelming business difficulties. 'It is very pleasant to reflect that he and John will frequently meet and talk of their absent friends', wrote Frederick to his mother after receiving a cheerful letter written during Bowring's outward journey. 'My father requires an active life to keep him in health and we may rejoice at his position freed from anxieties of a life in London. When he has once put things into a little order at Canton and become initiated in his duties, we shall doubtless have very pleasant letters from him' (11 March 1849). Frederick hoped that his father's increased leisure at Canton would enable him to resume his literary activities. 'If he were to be for some time disengaged from the political business of life, he would, I am convinced, return to his ancient favourite, the nymph poetry, which he used to cultivate with so much love and success. It seems strange and yet at the same time natural, that change of scene should have brought back the train of thought which produced the best of his hymns and *Matins and Vespers*' (1 April 1849). Bowring's wife shared her son's optimism. 'Your father must have been delighted and cheered by the kind and grateful present of the Maltese', she wrote, 'how richly he deserves the kindnesses he meets. There is a great debt of gratitude in the world and I can speak warmly of good friends and faithful friends for I have many in whom I have the most faithful trust' (19 February 1849).

When Bowring arrived at Canton in April 1849, however, he soon became disillusioned with the situation and bitterly regretted that he had ever left England. The circumstances at the Chinese city were parlous indeed. The consular system had been established less than ten years and in spite of treaty agreements reached at Nanking, 'foreign barbarians' were still not allowed by the Chinese authorities to enter the walled city and were restricted to the dismal area of the foreign compounds occupied by European merchants, sailors and missionaries. In spite of a previous agreement to do so, the Imperial Commissioner refused to receive Bowring within the city. After his busy political and literary life in England, Bowring found he had little in common with most of the merchants, who spent their time endlessly discussing business affairs and indulging in frivolous pastimes. The other consular officials were hardly better company than the merchants. There was, indeed, John in the service of Jardine Matheson and Co. at what Bowring called the 'barren rock' of Hong Kong, where Sir George Bonham, the British Plenipotentiary, (a younger man than Bowring), now had his headquarters, but Hong Kong was nearly eighty miles down river from Canton and Bowring saw little of his son. On the day of his arrival he was, he informed Edgar, 'overcome with a feeling of loneliness. I contrasted my domicile here with the house I had left . . . for Canton is absolutely and truly a prison – with no access to the town – and the Europeans incarcerated in the factories and the two gardens in front of them before the river. As my duty has placed me here', he added, 'I have made up my mind to make the best of it – bearing my exile and forbearing to complain of a fate of my own devising' (12 April 1849). In this mood of resignation he attempted to get down to his consular duties, but he soon discovered that even in his routine tasks there was much to discourage him. 'I do not believe that ten per cent of the revenues reach the Imperial Treasury', he complained to Edgar, 'every day I have some new evidence of the universal corruption . . . and if ever Peking is reached it will be found an Augean stable of corruption beyond anything that has entered into man's imagination'

(17 December 1849). Bowring, however, was too resilient to be over-whelmed by circumstances for long. As his knowledge of the local language improved, he began to cultivate the acquaintance of the local people, taking solitary walks in the neighbourhood of the Canton factories and purchasing Eastern curios which he despatched to his family and friends in England. 'I devote myself to Chinese studies', he wrote, 'in the dream that I may be called to a wider field of interest here – if not – I may perhaps write a book upon China and contribute something to the field of human knowledge. I have seen something nobody else has seen – and have my own views with respect to Chinese matters' (16 April 1850).

In October 1850 came a break in the monotony when Bowring received three months' leave and went on tour of the other treaty ports. Shanghai in particular impressed him by the rapid growth of its commercial importance. But by early 1851 he was back at Canton where his sense of frustration returned, particularly as this was the year of the Great Exhibition and Edgar, at the Board of Trade, had been made acting secretary to the Exhibition commission, a position which brought him into contact with the Prince Consort himself. An attempt by Bowring to organise a display of Eastern wares to send to the Crystal Palace was frustrated by the indifference of the merchants.

The difficulties of Bowring in China were increased by problems at home, where Edgar and Bowring's brother, Charles, were sorting out the debts of the Llynvi Iron Company and Bowring's other investments; though Edgar had successfully disposed of the lease of the property at Queen's Square. Most disturbing of these problems was the future of Bowring's son Charles, whom Bowring was now trying to get out to Canton as vice-consul, where he would be 'under my own eye'. 'He told me two years ago', he wrote to Frederick, 'that he did not know if he should be able to subscribe to the thirty-nine articles . . . I understood by this that he had not fully abandoned Unitarian doctrines but never dreamed of his approaching Catholic-ism. But he is by nature taciturn – referring questions rather to the solution of his own mind than to the authority of others. Charles has a strong intelligence – but I fear weak sympathies' (20 April 1849).

The future of Charles had in fact dominated the thoughts of all the family since Bowring had left England and much of Frederick's correspondence was concerned with this matter, not least because

Charles's conversion to Catholicism made it impossible for him to complete his studies at Cambridge, where the authorities were fearful of 'the dangerous example [Charles's] action would hold out to the undergraduates'. 'You may imagine my own position is just at present not the pleasantest possible', Frederick explained to his mother, 'the news having spread very rapidly and I have already been bored with numberless questions. However, I say but little – we must now make the best of a bad matter. I have now more than ever reason to be glad that Charles did not return to Cambridge. It would have been very unpleasant for him and of no earthly use' (29 January 1849). Frederick's mother, writing on 19 February 1849 after Charles had visited Exeter, confessed that her son's conversion and withdrawal from the university was 'a terrible disappointment to me':

He was baptised on Saturday and has since been troubling himself about taking a new name at Confirmation which is the usual practice. He is more completely a Roman Catholic than I could have believed possible . . . He intends to eat dry bread on the fast days. I have advised him to try vegetables and puddings, if he may not eat meat. He will no longer join in our evening prayers. I do not look on this quite as your aunts do for I confess it does not seem any more wonderful than the unwillingness they or Maria would feel in going to Church with me. I am sorry for it, however, I regret much everything that can make separation between members of a family. How a mind like his could be so enslaved by Priests and Traditions I cannot imagine. He is so good a fellow that we must take comfort even whilst smarting under so severe a disappointment.

Frederick wrote a mournful letter (17 January 1849) to his mother, confessing that 'though I have long expected something of the kind, it was a bitter pang to see it'.

It does but realise my first fears that if Charles should become a Roman Catholic, he would take the extremist views. He thinks them right and true and is prepared to carry them out, how he does not exactly say, probably he does not as yet feel conscious if the end is to be active or passive, meditating or proselytizing, in England or Italy, Europe or Asia . . . One useful lesson of all this unhappy affair teaches us that we who are left should draw nearer to you, my father and each other, in the bonds of filial and fraternal love. All will not be broken.

The future intentions of Charles now became a matter of concern for the whole family. For a time he became tutor to a Catholic family in Dover, where Frederick found him 'getting on comfortably in his new position'. His father had few doubts that if his efforts to secure office for his son in China should be unsuccessful, Charles would certainly enter the Catholic priesthood. In a letter to Edgar, who was inclined to take a more sympathetic view of his younger brother than Frederick did – Bowring had gently reminded Frederick that a few years earlier he 'had had to pass through the same (to me very sad) valley of tears' in Frederick's and Maria's own case – he wrote, 'I will not bind his conscience and convictions with a rod of iron. I have no such right. My grief should not interfere with what he thinks a call of duty. And I entreat you – I enjoin you all – as far as paternal affection can entreat or enjoin – that your love may not be alienated from this my youngest son and your youngest brother – blame him not – the world will pour enough of censure upon his head' (19 April 1849). 'I wish he would fall in love', he confessed to Edgar in a later letter, 'that would be his salvation – but I know not if he has any of the material in him out of which Cupid makes his martyrs – you are none of you very inflammable. Even you might now be looking around' (24 November 1849).

On Christmas Eve 1849 Bowring was, therefore, delighted to receive from Bonham the news that Palmerston had instructed that Charles should be given the first vacant vice-consulship in China. In spite of Bowring's loneliness, which in Frederick's words 'makes his affectionate nature yearn for home and friends to an almost painful degree' (3 November 1849), a wave of optimism now swept over him. 'As I see things going on so well at home', he assured Frederick, 'I shall live on very tranquilly here. I can promise you all that your mother and the Larkbear family shall be comfortably provided for and something more. And we must hope for a revival of the iron trade in two or three years. I too may turn my face towards home. I am getting more at home here. I go about in all directions' (22 November 1849).

A month or so after this, Bowring received the news that Charles had rejected Palmerston's offer and had decided to take up a novitiate at the Jesuit College at Stonyhurst. Coinciding as this did with the news that, in spite of his brother Charles's optimism, his bonds in the Llynvi Iron Company had been cancelled, Bowring's dreams collapsed and he was moved almost to despair. As he wrote to Edgar (21 November 1850):

The conduct of the company I consider an intolerable injustice, cruelty and oppression. I consider that each of my children is pillaged of nearly £2000. I think they have used their power as reckless tyrants use it. I now grieve that I ever left England – to be humiliated and scorned here – and to see my property plundered and confiscated in my absence ... At such – and so sad – so dark – so desolute a moment – in this my absolute solitude and seclusion – when I contemplate the wreck and ruin caused by arbitrary peremptoriness and cold hearted extortion – in such a moment this visit of Charles from his Jesuitical hiding place comes to haunt and to harrass me. I fed upon the faint dreaming that Lord Palmerston's kindness would have been known to you and that Charles would have yielded himself becomingly to the promise he made – it came from himself – it was spontaneous and voluntary – that if Lord Palmerston give him an appointment that appointment he would accept – and now I fear (horrible fear) that he will plead it comes too late ... I see by the confessions in Charles's letters – that he is not – and for a long time has not been – in his own hands – that he is now a puppet moved by strings which he calls 'conscience' and 'religion' and that these strings are pulled by dexterous intriguers and plotting 'Fathers', to such I will not willingly give him over. If Charles proceeds it must be now in disobedience to and in defiance of my wishes and prayers. I feel so forlorn and abandoned that I have heart for nothing. The truth is my sun is fast declining and the infirmities of age intellectual and physical make their gradual inroads. My only link to life now is my children's happiness – if that be severed I feel that I may be mangled and lost in the things that were and have ceased to be ... I am nothing and nobody – a custom house tide master to the Chinese – seeing all my superiors robbing the revenue.

In England Charles's decision to become a Jesuit had been known several months earlier and drew from Frederick the opinion 'that he would be an intensely bigoted priest and act upon the extremist maxims of any order he should happen to join' (1 December 1849). 'My father is immensely mistaken in thinking Charles would ever make a figure in the Roman Catholic Church', he assured his mother. 'He would I doubt not be a learned, virtuous and contented priest but not a successful one – that requires qualities he does not possess'. (Here Frederick was echoing the opinions of his two Larkbear aunts, who considered Charles's convictions as evidence of some intellectual infirmity.) As for Palmerston's rejected offer, 'it would have given him an ample income with considerable means of assisting the family and that ought to be no slight consideration. Edgar tells me', added Frederick, 'he has written to Charles on the subject but evidently does not expect his appeal will do much' (24 February 1850). In letter after letter to both his parents, Frederick, the Low Church Anglican, dwelt on his brother's decision to become a Jesuit, admitting that he seems to act from high principles, 'which we must not oppose though I can only regret that so fine a face should be shaded by a monk's cowl' (22 November 1850). To his mother's fears that Jesuitical influences would harden her son's heart, Frederick replied with an outburst of indignation worthy of his father:

He seems to lament that the discipline is not more stringent – to long for less sleep – less eating, less talking (than an hour per diem!) together with an iron-spiked bed or a couple of cudgelings per diem. From the moment Charles became a Roman Catholic I looked upon him as severed from his family practically for ever ... I cannot but believe him to be unconsciously the slave of a degrading superstition, his ecstatic visions – idle dreams – his obedience – voluntary servitude – his only possible career – not truth, freedom, eternity – but falsehood, imposture, perishable and perishing system. But we have this comfort; it is not we who have severed ourselves from him in his journey to another faith – but he who has severed himself from us – with the Roman Catholics, the acme of merit, with me, the most decisive condemnation of their faith. I am not so much a bigot in my own faith as to think that Emily [who had now become an Anglican like her eldest sister] ought to have become a member of it at all hazards (though of course, I am glad she is such) but I think both you and my father will agree that to have one child in the family a Roman Catholic is bitter experience enough – and that was the only alternative.

Little is recorded about the reactions of other relations of the family to Charles's religious change. A letter from Charles's uncle, Thomas Ward, to the Unitarian minister, Joseph Hunter, is therefore of interest. 'I hear nothing of my nephew Bowring, the Jesuit', he wrote, 'do you? Well after all, it is a pity people cannot worship as they please, without hindrance.'

As the furore over Charles's conversion began to subside, signs of another dispute began to reach Bowring at Canton. Tension at Larkbear between Bowring's wife and his two unmarried sisters had developed, partly over their criticisms of Charles's 'infirmity', partly over the desire of Bowring's wife not unnaturally to be mistress of her own home. It was Edgar, rather than Frederick, (whose adoring aunts still wrote to him regularly), who first informed his father that trouble was brewing. Bowring sent a somewhat touchy reply. 'As to your mother's quitting Exeter, it is out of the question. I cannot think of two establishments. I wish her, as far as a moderate expenditure goes, to visit her friends. She has unhappy prejudices against Larkbear and the Larkbearians and must be judged kindly and indulgently considering her situation and mine – but she will not turn my arrangements topsy-turvy – nor follow, I hope any injudicious counsels. People always like those who say "ditto" to all they say – however prejudiced it may be – and your mother is not free from the common failure' (4 June 1849).

With increasing tension at Exeter and the collapse of the China plans for his son Charles, Bowring began to consider ways for other members of his family to join him at Canton. The idea that his brother Charles should take his son's place as vice-consul seems to have come first from Bowring's sisters and was taken up eagerly by Frederick and by Charles himself, who 'in his usual cheerful and hopeful spirit' had been over-optimistic about the recovery of the Llynvi Iron Company. 'I shall only say that I hear Uncle Charles's position in the Llynvi Co. has become anything but a pleasant one', Frederick wrote to his father, 'and that he will be thrown in September on his own resources. He says he would like such a post extremely and readily accept it. I think he would fill it well and be a very great comfort to you, much more so than Charles the younger could have been' (17 March 1850). Bowring took up the suggestion eagerly and urged Edgar to press the Foreign Office for his uncle's appointment, suggesting that Charles 'bring out Maria and Emily with him – Edith cannot be separated from her mother . . . If we carry this out we should establish here a comfortable family party . . . and we might look to Charles taking my place when I returned home. I should be a different man had I a family around me . . . As to your mother I would have her comfort and her wishes consulted. She pines to be mistress somewhere and though I have as you all know resisted the schemes for her leaving Larkbear, I think her leaving it would be right and reasonable if two of my daughters came to China . . .' (17 July 1850). In the end, however, these plans came to nothing, ostensibly on the grounds that Bowring saw 'no present prospect of a vacancy' at Canton. Edgar probably had difficulty in persuading the authorities to transfer the appointment to his uncle after his brother Charles's rejection of it.

The failure must have been a disappointment both to Bowring and his brother and to Frederick, who had a warm affection for his uncle, lasting from his childhood days at Exeter. He still went on walking holidays with Charles in the Welsh mountains. 'I saw the portrait taken of my father the other day', Frederick informed his mother in 1851, 'I always fancied my father and uncle Charles the two brothers most unlike in the world. The portrait really makes him like uncle Charles, broad-faced as he is. It is really very surprising, at least so it struck me' (3 November 1851). This affection for her brother-in-law was not apparently shared by Bowring's wife. 'I wish my mother would not write to me as she does about Uncle Charles', Frederick complained to his father some years later. 'She does not in the least understand his character and does him great injustice and it both hurts and annoys me' (1 June 1856).

There is no need to reiterate in detail the expressions of self-pity which overwhelmed Bowring whenever he returned to Canton and usually dispersed when he was able to leave it. 'Remember what is for a man with my habits to be condemned to imprisonment – isolation – no conversation about books – no politics – no sympathy – no friendship' (28 January 1851). 'He writes as if depressed which I cannot wonder at', wrote Frederick to his mother, 'as if he longed to return to Europe which I cannot wonder at either, though it is absolutely essential that he should remain where he is at present. To come home would be to expose himself to the greatest annoyance and the mortifications attendant on a very small income. Would that he were twenty years younger. At nearly 60 after a stormy life one cannot expect the same indifference to foreign lands and absence from home as in the prime of life he would have shown' (24 November 1851).

In his isolation from wife and family, Bowring's thoughts turned again to the future domestic happiness of his sons, perhaps induced by the realisation that his Jesuit son Charles would now never get married. 'Surely you might be a much happier man with a wife and a home', he wrote to Edgar, 'you might find some lady who would join her fortunes to yours – and give me one more being at least to love . . . Habits of bachelorship grow – and men and women as they grow older less easily accord themselves to others. Lewin says he shall wait until he goes home – and perhaps this is very prudent – and John is not likely to link himself to anything that China can offer . . . Frederick, no doubt, would like to feel himself properly launched – which is reasonable for he will have to make a sacrifice if he marry before his Fellowship expires' (February 1851). In a later letter to Edgar (26 May 1851) he wrote more pressingly:

I do attribute all the main sources of my happiness to my having settled – as it is called – when young. This – with the kind providence of God – has enabled me to see my children placed in positions whence they can make their own way in the world – and make their way, I trust, without being scratched by so many briars and thorns – and tumbling on so many rough stones – as has been the lot of their father – whose children have been to him the stars above and the flowers below. I do not want you to make an ambitious marriage – but a prudent and above all a happy one. The truth is your location at home give you many facilities which your wandering brothers do not share – Fritz must want to be married, I expect, to his Fellowship as long as it lasts.

Frederick who, after careful consideration, had decided to give up his fellowship and move into chambers at Lincoln's Inn, had already received similar advice from Bowring on his leaving Cambridge. He was 'immensely amused at my father's anxiety to see a grandson or say *even* a granddaughter, of which there appears small chance indeed for many a year to come. He seems to speculate', he told his mother, 'whether his Chinese, his Indian, his official, or his legal grandson will first walk in sky blue coat and white trowsers (isn't that the style?) or whether the firstborn will be black, red or white and whether the indefinite "it" will turn into a definite "he" or definite "she". All the while his degenerate sons seem to think as little of the matter as if marriage and givings in marriage were things of another sphere ' (8 December 1850).

In the following year, Edgar, on whom the pressure to marry was strongest, informed his father of his engagement to Colonel Thompson's daughter, Lily. Bowring was overjoyed and despatched present after present to his son and future daughter-in-law; dresses, cushions, 'an embroidered table cover for your drawing-room when you have one' and many Eastern curios. The excitement, however, was short-lived, for in December 1852 he received news that Edgar's engagement to Lily Thompson had been broken off. Edgar's letters to his disappointed father became more and more depressed. He intimated his intention of giving up his position at the Board of Trade, where his prospects of promotion had declined under a Tory government, and wrote about abandoning his duties as his father's business manager. Bowring himself tried to be philosophical about his son's personal misfortunes, urging Edgar to 'seek alliances elsewhere' and 'not to long for the inaccessible'. 'In this world', he reminded his son, 'most have experienced disappointments similar to this one' (10 December 1852). He was more disturbed, however, by Edgar's proposal to resign from the Board of Trade. This, he realised, might not only ruin his son's career but would break off one of his own main lines of private communication with the administration at home. 'I entreat you', he wrote 'on your love to me not to contemplate any surrender of your office' (23 January 1853). Bowring's advice was in this respect justified, for on the formation of Lord Aberdeen's coalition government in December 1852, Edgar again obtained preferment at the Board of Trade, being appointed registrar and also private secretary to Lord Stanley. The change of fortune restored his confidence in other ways, for a few months later he became engaged to Sophia Cubitt, daughter of the wealthy builder

Thomas Cubitt, who had been associated with him during the Great Exhibition. They were married in May 1853, shortly before Bowring's arrival back in England on leave and a year later, soon after Bowring's return to China, his first grandson, 'Edgarino', was born. 'By the time you have received this', wrote Bowring to his son in 1854, on board a battleship bound for Shanghai, 'I hope you will have entered on the parental relations – a great event – the great event of a man's history – for it is that which connects him with the future and establishes the link which binds him to something more than the world of shadows. The childless man passes soon into social and personal oblivion. His name unlisped – unuttered by his descendants soon passes away – but he whose memory is to be preserved by his offspring gives additional hostages to virtuous fame and will be more careful of his honourable reputation' (26 May 1854).

At the end of 1851 Bowring had taken another period of leave when he visited Ceylon and India. He met Lewin at Calcutta and 'had much intercourse with all the high officials' on relations between India and China, particularly on the opium question. While in India he received notice of his temporary appointment as Plenipotentiary at Hong Kong, during Bonham's leave. He also received reports of a fresh domestic crisis at Exeter, involving his eldest daughter, Maria. The roots of this affair went back to Maria's conversion to Anglicanism in 1842 and her attendance with her aunts at Exeter Cathedral. The Bishop of Exeter, Henry Phillpotts, was a man of formidable personality, a stout upholder of the rights of the Established Church, a strong and ruthless opponent of non-conformity and sympathetic to the Oxford Movement. In 1848, the daughter of a naval officer, Priscilla Sellon, who held strong Puseyite opinions in her religion and had the support of the Bishop of Exeter, established at Devonport a religious community, the Sisters of Mercy, providing help for aged sailors, prostitutes and destitute members of society. This organisation was viewed with grave suspicion by opponents of High Church Anglicanism, who accused Miss Sellon and her followers of trying to take advantage of the wealth of single women by encouraging them to join the community. It is not known exactly when Maria joined the Sisters and when she left them again, but her family were greatly disturbed. As early as 1849 Bowring was complaining about 'narrow-minded bigots' influencing his daughter. Maria's action provoked strong opposition both from her Unitarian mother and from her two

Anglican aunts, who confronted Miss Sellon in the cathedral, wrote to the bishop and took part in an angry correspondence in the local press. This fresh demonstration of what Bowring's wife considered the 'strange ways of new Christians' led to a revival of tension at Larkbear and increased her visits to her Lewin relations in London and elsewhere.

Taking place soon after Charles's conversion to Catholicism, this episode co-incided with increasing hostility amongst many Protestants both to the Catholic church and to the Anglo-Catholic movement – a hostility fanned by the re-establishment of a Roman Catholic hierarchy in England in 1850. 'I want no more family disruptions', wrote Bowring to Frederick from Colombo, 'but I cannot go further than denying my consent if Maria insist on her right to dispose of herself by this course of action – what can I do to prevent it? Perhaps it will wait – but religious passions – or tendencies fancying themselves religious – are sometimes unwilling to wait on my return home – I have written to her at length, but with great distrust of my powers of persuasion' (22 January 1852). In a number of letters written from Hong Kong to Frederick, whom he viewed as one of his sisters' 'own boys' who could deal with the Exeter situation more easily than Edgar, Bowring at last conceded that his wife and daughters might have another home provided for them, since his temporary appointment at Hong Kong had improved his salary. 'In their indignation against Miss Sellon', he wrote, 'your aunts have so much extended the publicity of these events . . . and Maria would at Exeter be so unhappily placed – the centre of so much notice and conversation – that I will not expose her to the consequent annoyance . . . and as regards your mother, I have not succeeded on my side in bringing about that forbearance . . . of the conduct and opinion of others which I have so earnestly sought to establish. At all events', wrote Bowring, (whose self-pitying manner was replaced by a somewhat Socratic tone after his transfer to Hong Kong as acting Plenipotentiary), 'I think it had better be considered that your mother's return to Exeter as her home, is negative'.

I shall consider I am to do what is right and fit towards my father and sisters – and no longer consider Larkbear as the general home. Maria sees her mistakes as clearly as any of us – and would bring the past in oblivion. I am exceedingly glad to observe how sensible a view you have taken. Your aunt Lucy says she has told her friends that had I been in England I would have raised the indignation of the whole county. No! No! I would have put my finger upon every lip and love for Maria herself would have led me to shelter her from the storms of public discussion – the very last thing to which a young lady should be exposed. As regards Larkbear you know I am only discharging a debt to my father – whose claims upon me have every character of urgency – gratitude – propriety – I ought to be indulgent – for I am hasty – sometimes intemperate – rash and reckless often – but I do not retain sources of discomfort – or wiilingly revert to past annoyances. (11 July 1852)

The Maria affair can be observed from a different angle in Frederick's letters to his mother. Not surprisingly it produced an outburst of wrath against the Puseyites. 'I think before long we shall find it necessary to abolish utterly all these (so called) religious houses, nunneries or "monkeries" ', he wrote, 'the best defence I have seen of them is (I think) Coleridge's, who says it is an outlet or escape valve for religious enthusiasm which would otherwise be constantly raising disturbances in the State . . . The nunneries of the Papists are silly enough in all conscience. This seems tomfoolery burlesqued' (4 January 1852). 'We ought to show that the family does not approve of Maria's proceedings', he added a week later, 'I should write to Maria kindly but firmly and let her feel how utterly opposed we all are to her senseless goings-on. As to Miss Sellon . . . I should simply require a definite explanation of the terms on which she considers Maria is staying at Plymouth' (11 January 1852). Frederick blamed Maria's actions on the influence of Charles, 'whose letters are just as natural as hers, as self-complacent and contented' (8 February 1852). 'Of course Maria like master Charles means to persevere in her wilful course. These saints always manage to have their own way and then dub it a "call" ' (23 March 1852). By the end of March, however, after Maria had returned to Larkbear, Frederick became seriously alarmed about the effects on Maria's sanity if she was not allowed to go back to Miss Sellon's establishment. As he wrote to his mother:

In ordinary circumstances, I certainly would not have appeared to countenance such an idea but if a daughter's or sister's happiness and health, and above all her reason, is at all likely to suffer from continued opposition, it is better at once to drop it and take a conciliatory view than to run so frightful a risk and I am quite sure that my father would never forgive us if we had thrown any opposition in the way and so distressing a result should take place. These high wrought religious, superstitious notions are very near madness and I feel easily become so; even if we greatly overrate the danger, it is our duty not to run it . . . My dear mother, I am sorry that you and my father should have another such sorrow as this seems likely to prove to be, nay is – but at Maria's age the dispositions are no longer pliable and the least painful course will be to yield at once.

In the end Maria decided not to go back to Devonport and it was decided not to talk to her about Miss Sellon or anything connected with the affair. It was not, however, the end of trouble, as Bowring's wife was still proposing to leave Larkbear, taking her daughters with her. Frederick was strongly opposed to the break-up of the family home and wrote from Exeter an impassioned letter (21 September 1852) to his father pointing out the harm such a rift would do not only to his grandfather and aunts but to his youngest sister, Emily, who adored Larkbear and was already showing signs of the troubles which lay ahead:

Her singularly sensitive and enthusiastic but clever nature is restrained and kept in order here, but is constantly irritated and made rebellious elsewhere. When she was on her visiting tour last year with my mother she was constantly ill, in tears and unhappy. Here she is the liveliest of creatures always well and industrious and happy and though she is not legally of age, she is very nearly so and quite able to judge what will be good for her. The plain truth must be told – my mother and Edith alone wish for the change and all the rest of us are most strongly opposed to it. I perhaps more than any as I am firmly convinced of the certain and necessary evils that it will bring with it and I regret to see that in my mother's plans no thought of what is due to my grandfather and aunts has entered. It should be remembered that this step is irrevocable and cannot be retraced . . . I never pretended to put the question of one or two houses as a mere question of pounds, shillings and pence. Every consideration seems to me to speak plainly for the former – comfort, convenience, respectability, economy. As to Maria, you can easily ascertain the truth from herself direct and the reality would soon be apparent. I hope you will consider things more calmly before you take a final resolve.

In the event, Bowring's return to England early in the following year, the serious illnesses of his two sisters and the decision of his wife and two elder daughters to return with him to China altered the situation and the separate household was never established. Meanwhile, Bowring, who strongly resisted a suggestion that the unhappy Maria might go out as a governess or companion, made to Frederick a concluding observation on the affair. 'It is indeed a sad pity that she did not marry and indeed, I feel it is a great mistake, if there be an opportunity, to delay that all important event. But girls have frequently little choice and little chance. And it is very difficult to see one's way where they are concerned. As to you', he urged Frederick, 'I would have no delay when you can marry and have found a desirable help mate' (23 December 1852).

It was about this time that Frederick, who was now established in chambers at Lincoln's Inn, had a visit from Charles, just after he had assured his mother that 'I do not think it would give me much pleasure to see Charles again, to me he would be utterly changed by the "brutalizing effects" of his training' (13 August 1852). 'I knew his odd knock directly', he wrote, 'he looks marvellously well and says he is very happy, his present studies of Logic and Rhetoric bringing him into communication with his favourite authors, are, I daresay, particularly agreeable to him ... I suspect from his studies that the Jesuits have found out that his gifts lie in teaching and mean to employ him in that way' (31 October 1852). In a second visit, Charles, who was later appointed Professor of Rhetoric at Stonyhurst, took tea with his elder brother and henceforth they seem to have kept regularly in touch until Charles's departure to the Jesuit College at Rome. 'To my surprise Charles called', noted Frederick in his diary early in 1854, 'dressed in a long black (ugly) cloak and enormous shoes'. By contrast with Charles, the earnest and hardworking Frederick was not happy with his slow progress as a barrister and wondered 'whether the Bar will really be so bad a profession as it promised to be'. Visits to Cambridge were disappointing as 'most, though not all of my old friends there have left it for ever and it is no longer the place to me which it was' (24 November 1852). He considered for a time going to Australia with a friend but gave it up, partly because of his father's return from China and the sad development in his grandfather's family at Exeter.

Early in 1853 Bonham arrived back at Hong Kong and Bowring, whose activities as acting Plenipotentiary had been restricted by the Tory government, resumed his consular duties at Canton. But after a brief stay at the factories, he was granted three months' leave and sailed to the Dutch East Indies. Here he was informed that an application he had made to return home on leave had been granted. No moment could have seemed more appropriate as he believed his chances of succeeding Bonham as Plenipotentiary were much increased now that the Whigs had returned to office and his old colleague, Lord Clarendon, was at the Foreign Office. Bowring arrived back at Southampton direct from Java in June 1853, nearly four and a half years after he had left the country. Even the claims of his family could not persuade him to remain settled for long and he was soon dashing around London with his old energy, trying to impress members of the government with his zeal for a more active policy in the Far East. In August he carried out a tour of the industrial north, describing the great opportunities in China to the Manchester Chamber of Commerce and other commercial associations. The northern people, he assured Clarendon, went 'wild with joy' on hearing about the vast new market open to their trade, declaring that if every Chinaman bought only a cotton night cap, all the mills would be kept going indefinitely. He also gave evidence before a parliamentary committee on decimal coinage and completed the preparation and publication of his book on this subject in association with his two sons and Augustus De Morgan, the London University mathematician. The American writer, Nathaniel Hawthorne, who encountered him at Liverpool, considered him a 'brisk person, with the address of a man of the world – free, quick to smile and of agreeable manners. He has a good face, rather American than English in aspect, and does not look above sixty . . . He talked in a lively way for 10 or 15 minutes and then took his leave, offering me any services in his power in London – as for instance to introduce me to the Athanaeum Club'. Both Frederick and Edgar were now members of their father's club and it was there that they often dined with him during his leave.

Meanwhile at Exeter Bowring found his two sisters both developing the mental illnesses which were to cloud their last years and put them for a time in an institution, while his father was becoming increasingly senile. Bowring's wife had returned from her relations to assist with the invalids and Edith was 'one of the best nurses'. 'It is a sad state of things', wrote Frederick, 'had it not been for this, how agreeable my father's stay in England would have been'. Moreover, Emily was now also turning from Anglicanism towards Roman Catholicism. 'Lewin [who was expected on leave from India] will exercise a beneficial influence upon the dear good girl', wrote Bowring to Frederick, 'but whether enough to emancipate her from Catholic trammels is doubtful. But it matters little. Charles and she have occult sympathies, one would think. I expect Charles will work his way as an erudite Jesuit to a position of some eminence' (January 1854).

In spite of his family problems, it was his chances of succeeding Bonham as Plenipotentiary in China which was uppermost in Bowring's mind. Indeed, Bonham had recommended him as his successor 'under proper instructions and restraints'. Bowring himself had written to Clarendon, putting forward his claims and also soliciting the consulship at Canton for Frederick on grounds that 'laborious habits, great knowledge of languages and a legal training particularly suited him for the post'. Clarendon, who was preoccupied with the diplomatic crisis in the Near East, had little time to concern himself with Chinese affairs and he referred Bowring's letter to the Chief Clerk at the Foreign Office, Edward Hammond, who gave an unenthusiastic appraisal of Bowring's claims to succeed Bonham. 'Of his talent and intellectual vivacity', he warned the Foreign Secretary, 'there can be no doubt but there might possibly be a question of his carrying sufficient ballast to countervail his superfluity of sail . . . He would probably be over the Great Wall before we had time to look around us'. In spite of Hammond's warning, Clarendon finally decided to appoint Bowring as Plenipotentiary and Chief Superintendent of Trade in the Far East; eventually his duties were extended to include the Governorship of Hong Kong as well. Clarendon probably believed that Bowring's appointment would please the radical wing in Parliament, on whose good will the coalition government partly depended. But he warned Bowring not to overstrain the claims of friendship by soliciting consulships in China for members of his family. He also agreed, under pressure from Ellice and Hume, whose goodwill towards Bowring had never wavered, to recommend him for a knighthood in order to enhance his prestige among the Chinese.

A month or so before Bowring was due to return, Frederick was informed by his mother that she wished to go to China with his father. 'I do not know how you could bear the journey', he wrote, 'and still more the intense summer heat there but if you think you and my father can raise the necessary money and outfit for you all, I do not see why you and Maria and Edith should not accompany him if you all wish it. But can proper arrangements be made for the comfort of my grandfather for that is a very essential part of the arrangement at his age? I am very much perplexed to know what to do as to writing to Aunt Lucy. I should wish to write if I could do any good or if it would give her any pleasure' (28 November 1853). 'The accounts seem on the whole favourable', he wrote a few weeks later, 'I do not despair of the *ultimate* recovery of both my poor aunts. What do you propose to do with Emily? I believe Uncle Charles [at Liverpool]. would be most happy to take her in until matters change for the better. It will be very lonely for my grandfather when all are gone, yet he would not care for or like change of place, I believe' (26 December 1853).

At the beginning of January 1854, Bowring made a rapid visit to Paris, accompanied by Frederick. They encountered unpleasant conditions on the railways in both countries because of heavy snow and Bowring returned with a cold. 'I beg him to stay at home for a few days and nurse his cold', Frederick wrote to his mother at Exeter, 'whereas he wants to be dashing about here, there and everywhere to no end'. On 16 February Bowring received his Knighthood from Queen Victoria and dined on the following day with all the members of his family, except Emily and Charles, at the Athenaeum. Next day 'Uncle Tom, Edgar, Sophia, her brother, Herbert Lewin [Bowring's wife's young nephew] and self', wrote Frederick in his diary, 'went to see our travellers off by the 3.00 p.m. train to Southampton. They all looked well except my father, who was much fagged'.

6

Sir John in Trouble

Bowring's situation in China was now very different from what it had been on the previous tour. He had his wife – now Lady Bowring – two of his daughters and his eldest son, John, with him and was soon joined by Lewin, who met the family at Colombo and accompanied his father on his mission to northern China. Bowring's responsibilities were considerable and took him first to Shanghai, the most successful of the treaty ports, to try to settle a complicated dispute over the payment of customs duties to the Chinese and then to the Peiho river, where he attempted in vain to persuade the Imperial authorities to allow him to continue up river to Peking. A visit to Canton was equally unrewarding, as the Imperial Commissioner, Yeh Ming-Ch'en, took as imperious a line as his predecessors to meeting the 'barbarian' Plenipotentiary. In 1855 Bowring sailed in a warship – appropriately named the *Rattler* – to Siam, accompanied by his son John and the determined young consul of Amoy, Harry Parkes, destined to have a distinguished career in the Far East. Bowring and Parkes successfully negotiated a commercial treaty with King Mongkut, who shared Bowring's interest in Western technical advances and was impressed by the doctoral gown which the new Plenipotentiary had brought out to China with him. The agreement was accompanied by elaborate ceremonies and the lavish exchange of gifts, but was as much due to the presence of the warship and the ruthless determination of Parkes as to Bowring's diplomacy. The visit was recorded in a diary kept by Bowring and, with additional information about the country, was published under the title *The Kingdom and People of Siam*. Bowring's two daughters had the task of preparing the book for publication and it was then sent home for Frederick and Edgar to see through the press. It proved to be one of the most successful of Bowring's books and has been republished in recent years as a detailed description of what was, at the time, a little-known Asiatic country.

The Siamese Treaty provoked strong opposition in England both from Lord Shaftesbury and from Bowring's radical friends because of clauses facilitating the free importation of opium into Siam. Of unauthorised opium smuggling into China, which actually increased after the Treaty of Nanking (1842), Bowring, at the time he was an MP, had been a strong critic. Since his arrival in the Far East, however, he had modified his views, ostensibly because of the difficulty of controlling the traffic. The question was, in fact, of peculiar embarrassment to him because of his own connections with Jardine Matheson and Co., who were the largest dealers in opium in the Far East. Not only was his son John, who had once been passed over for promotion, now a partner in Jardine Matheson but he himself had obligations to the firm, which acted as his bankers in China, advanced him loans during his years of penury after 1848 and alone supported his policy on arrears duties at Shanghai. Bowring's enemies were well aware of the circumstances which obliged him to 'deal daintily' with Jardine Matheson. Some of the merchants had written a 'violent diatribe' to Palmerston, accusing Bowring of being biased against the commercial community and demanding his recall. Similar charges of having sold himself to opium merchants were again to be made against Bowring after the outbreak of war at Canton.

As it was impossible to consider more determined methods of enforcing the 1842 Treaty of Nanking while the Crimean War was continuing, Bowring began to give attention to the administration of Hong Kong, which had already caused his predecessors considerable problems. As a result of his unsuccessful attempts to enforce the payment of arrears duties at Shanghai, he had become extremely unpopular with the British merchants in China and their commercial supporters in England, obliging both Edgar and Lewin to write to the *Times* defending their father against attack. Bowring's attempts to reform the corrupt and crime-ridden colony of Hong Kong and to end lucrative monopolies also brought him many enemies, including the influential *Friend of China*, which had at first welcomed his appointment. No doubt his sense of self-importance had been increased by his knighthood. 'Our chief does not impress anyone with anything but a restless desire for a movement around the centre of his own kudos', complained one of his staff, 'and you can see at

John Bowring Esq LLD Governor of Hong Kong. *Illustrated London News*, February 18, 1854

once that the people in contact soon get their noses up'. Faced with so much opposition both from the merchants and from the Chinese authorities and receiving little support from the government at home, which considered he had acted unwisely over the customs duties dispute, Bowring began to show a belligerent tone in his correspondence, as previously when he had run into opposition in France and elsewhere. He had returned to China full of confidence in his ability to handle the Imperial authorities more successfully than his predecessors had done. 'My old age will be crowned with the glory of having rendered services more important in the field of peace than the conqueror can effect in war', he had written to Edgar (17 July 1854), adding in a later letter that he was 'not without hope that you will hear from me under the date of Peking ... this is quite upon the cards and if we get there, be assured we shall do something' (7 October 1854).

After the failure at the Peiho river, however, and the rebuff at Canton, Bowring admitted that he was 'exhausting patience with these stubborn mandarins' (25 December 1854). To Hammond at the Foreign Office he wrote more bluntly than to his son: 'it is hard to get on with these stubborn mandarins. Before long I am afraid we shall have to employ something harder than brain bullets'. The success in Siam further bolstered his confidence and increased his determination to penetrate China, which he saw as an important market for British manufacturers, counterbalancing the traditional annual export from China of tea and silk and replacing the financial dependence of British merchants on the opium trade. While still at Bangkok he had urged Clarendon to allow him to 'open China' as he had opened Siam, with the 'instruments of peace' in his hand but with 'a co-operative naval force' under his command. After his return to Hong Kong his demands for a forceful policy became increasingly insistent. Two years later, after this policy had got Bowring into trouble, he went to considerable lengths to declare his disapproval of 'strong language and a sloop of war to support it', reminding everyone of his lifelong membership of the Peace Society. In 1855 and 1856, however, there was little either in his official despatches to the Foreign Office or in his private letters to suggest that he ever hesitated to recommend violent means if these would help to secure the great objective of opening China to European commerce. 'We have been trifled with – tantalized – too long', he wrote to Clarendon late in 1855, 'a natural result of our temporizing and hesitation – to suppose that our motives have been understood . . . is to be ignorant of the oriental mind – that mind never distinguishes between the will to do – and the power of doing – never attributes forbearance to anything but impotence or dreams that hesitations can have any source but a sense of infirmity'.

During the years following Bowring's return to China, when he had little time to think about family problems in England, his two sisters and father had continued to deteriorate. At Larkbear the only member of the family then residing (apart from an aged relation to Bowring's mother in a nearby cottage – 'Aunt Lane') was Emily, though she was joined late in 1854 by Lewin on leave from India. Emily was now, like Maria before her, proposing to enter a convent, an action to which Bowring and his wife were strongly opposed. 'I need scarcely say that Emily is as completely fanatical and wrapped up in the one subject of her religion and its real and supposed duties, as a person can well be', wrote Frederick. 'I think she at first dreaded Lewin's arrival but now she gets on better with him than anyone and it was amusing to see how Lewin hated her being out of sight. I think it is not unlikely that Lewin will meet with a good deal of attention from people, particularly as he is so cool and possessed in the society of other people ... which could never be said of me' (12 November 1854). When it was that Frederick discovered that Lewin, far from emancipating his sister 'from Catholic trammels', had himself turned to Roman Catholicism, is unrecorded but his parents were aware of the situation by the end of 1855. 'Emily seems very happy', wrote Frederick, 'and what with her religious duties and her school and visits to the poor, she never seems idle'. Lewin and Emily 'appear to be more closely allied than ever since he became a Roman Catholic. I cannot say it gives me much pleasure but no doubt to Emily and Charles it was a source of unmixed pleasure ... As my grandfather and Aunt Lucy do not get up in the morning to breakfast, it is rather a lonely meal for her. I am not sure, however, that she minds it, for she always goes to church before breakfast and that and her school occupy her mind principally' (10 October 1855). 'I can by no means understand Lewin's aberrations', wrote Bowring to Frederick, 'I should find perhaps no stronger predisposing cause than his sympathy with Emily. Lewin's brotherhood with Charles will also be greatly strengthened by his religious change. I forget whether they have met since Lewin's return to England. I wish earnestly that Lewin would take a look into himself' (16 December 1855).

It was about a week after this letter was written that Bowring's elder sister Anne died, probably in an institution. She was followed to her grave by Lucy, who died at Larkbear early in the following year. What exactly the mental malady was from which they suffered is difficult to determine. 'Aunt Lucy ... though in Aunt Anne's presence she shows admirable fortitude, yet when alone her very soul seems rent and torn with alternate agonies of hope and fear', Frederick had written in 1853 (16 August 1853). 'I have just received from Aunt Lucy a touching and painful letter in which she complains of the hopelessness of her state and of the certainty that she should shortly be strictly confined. Her letter was long but unrelieved by any hopeful expression or cheering thought of any kind', (17 December 1853). A few months before her death Bowring had been informed that Lucy had also become a Roman Catholic. Bowring took this news more calmly than the conversions in his own family. 'If poor Lucy found comfort in the change', he wrote to Edgar, 'that comfort would be my consolation. I love her not less for her altered faith. Why should I? – especially as I attach less and less importance to types of creed. I value more and more the veritable graces of the Christian character. 'To do the Will of God' is worth a million credos and any amount of sacrificial or other outward observancies' (2 December 1855). On the news of her death a few months later Bowring was 'grateful that the perturbed spirit is no longer troubled. I cannot but feel the blank and mourn the loss of one I loved and who loved me so well', he wrote to Edgar (November 1856). The death of Lucy and of Bowring's father, on the day after Lucy's funeral, was described by Frederick in a long letter to his parents (8 April 1856):

> I was with her to within a few seconds of her last gasp and had only flown next door to desire my Aunt Lane to come quickly, when on return the news met us that she was gone ... Her funeral took place last Thursday according to the rites of her Church and what they call a High Mass was celebrated which gratified Emily and Lewin who attribute great efficacy to it ... My grandfather suffered no pain whatever; on the Thursday when I wished him goodbye on my leaving after the funeral of Aunt Lucy he said, 'Goodbye Fritz' and the placid brow he then showed was unchanged when I saw him in his coffin on Saturday night. There was no sign of pain or emotion – he might have been sleeping. He was buried in the same grave with Aunt Lucy ... This home is now desolate and what that means is known only to Lewin and myself whose home it was for so long.

Frederick wrote later (1 June 1856) that 'poor Emily had sad fits of hysteria for some days after the funeral and I was exceedingly glad when she and Lewin formed a determination to leave Exeter for a short time'.

This news reached Bowring at Hong Kong towards the end of April: 'nor do I desire the prolongation of an existence which seems reduced to the mere exercise of the animal functions', he wrote of his father's death. 'As to poor Lucy – there we see release from inconceivable hopeless pain. These are matters of awful mystery'. The deaths were briefly reported in a local Exeter newspaper, according to which 'both sisters who had been constant attendants at the cathedral and were well known in this city, being somewhat eccentric in their habits, had left Exeter some time before their deaths. Since then the deceased [Lucy] had become a Roman Catholic and was received into communion with that body'.

On the news of the deaths of Bowring's father and sisters, his son John was somewhat grudgingly given leave by Jardine Matheson to visit England to settle affairs at Larkbear with Frederick and Edgar. By the summer of 1856 John was back in England, where Frederick considered 'he looked so thin and weak, all skin and bone. He could then hardly stand upright' (29 July 1856). By the autumn, however, he had recovered. 'John is a universal favourite with all of us, indeed with everybody', Frederick wrote to his father. 'He is generous, kind, thoughtful and uncomplaining. We all rejoice in his prosperity, which seems this year, indeed, to be something great' (17 October 1856). Arrangements were made between the brothers for Larkbear to be let. Lewin got married during his leave to Mary Talbot, a daughter of Admiral John Talbot. His wife returned with him to India and Emily came out to China with her eldest brother, John.

During this period Frederick, who was an admirer of J. S. Mill (with whom Bowring's own relations always remained cool), wrote regularly to his father about the political and literary events of the day, sending him the latest books (including *Jane Eyre* and *Wuthering Heights*) and telling him the latest news. He assured his father that he was at last making progress at the Bar. 'I really begin to think I am getting on', he wrote, 'I mean in reputation, for briefs have not been numerous. I believe my slow way of going to work will prove the quickest in the end'. Bowring, who probably was correct in regarding his son's unwillingness to move into the world as his besetting sin, his *vis inertia*, was 'much pleased with your accounts of your studies and prospects'. As he wrote (5 April 1856), perhaps recalling Bentham:

I want to see you in that part of the law where you will find most exercise for the higher principles of equity and philosophy. How I should rejoice to see a veritably good book on International Law from your pen. My mind has always been too

95

desultory – my knowledge too superficial – experience has taught me something in the management of affairs and I think I have some aptitude for diplomatic business – not by artful devices or trickery – nor concealment of purpose – but by a good deal of natural frankness – which may sometimes get me into scrapes – but which in the long run is appreciated at its true value.

The best-known example of Bowring's diplomacy getting him into a scrape occurred a few months after this letter to Frederick. Following the boarding by Chinese soldiers of a British-registered light vessel, the lorcha *Arrow* in the Pearl River on 8 October 1856 and what was considered an inadequate explanation of the incident by the Imperial Commissioner, Yeh, Bowring authorised the despatch of a naval force under Admiral Seymour, the bombardment of Canton and the forcible entrance into that city by Parkes. Bowring had recently advised Clarendon that the demand for his reception by the Commissioner 'must be made in the presence of ships of war' and had assured him that there would only be a nominal show of resistance. An account of this well-known and – to Bowring – disastrous action was given in a letter to Edgar; 'the *vexata questio* left unsolved by all my predecessors, I have satisfactorily settled and with a very small loss our naval forces have entered the city of Canton. I think this mode of action more worthy of a Great Nation than the stoppage of duties and disturbance of trade – out of these troubled waters I expect to extract some healing food' (16 October 1856). Unfortunately for Bowring the lack of military forces to support the naval attack made it impossible for Parkes to hold on to the city and consolidate his position and strengthened the determination of Yeh to resist the invaders. During the following weeks the Chinese directed several attacks against the British in the neighbourhood of Canton. On 14 December Chinese 'braves' set on fire and destroyed the European quarter of the factories, gutting the consulate and causing the death of a young nephew of Bowring's on his mother's side, whom he had appointed as a consular assistant. In the following week raids were made by war junks on vessels lying in the river, culminating in the massacre of all Europeans on board a postal steamer on its way from Canton to Hong Kong.

The emergency reached its climax on 11 January 1857, when an attempt was made to poison the European population of Hong Kong

96

by putting arsenic in their bread. About 300–400 people were affected. Fortunately for Bowring and his family and the other members of the European community, the poisoners made the mistake of overdoing the arsenic and their victims suffered little worse than severe attacks of sickness. The incident caused the greatest alarm and, together with the appearance of posters offering rewards for the heads of Europeans, scared the administration into taking strong measures against the Chinese. Eventually after Bowring, to his credit, had refused martial law and insisted on a proper trial, the baker of the poisoned bread and other suspects were acquitted for lack of evidence and allowed to leave the colony. Meanwhile Bowring sent out appeals for military reinforcements from India and Singapore and assured the Foreign Secretary of his determination to continue his forward policy in China in spite of temporary setbacks. 'We, of course, are a good deal inconvenienced by the desertion of our servants . . . their families being menaced by the most terrible threats', he wrote to Edgar, 'enormous sums are publicly voted by the people for anyone who will burn our city. I scarcely dare tell you how much your father's head would produce but certainly a large fortune to its owner – if its owner were anybody but he who bears it on his shoulders. We take very energetic measures – and though we have a "shocking bad" population – the ruffianism of southern China – in our island, I still hope we shall pass through the crisis without much peril' (10 January 1857).

The first reports of the attack on Canton reached London early in 1857, with public reaction varying from enthusiasm for war with China to strong indignation over Bowring's conduct. Most members of the government, whatever their private reservations on the way in which the conflict had come about, shared Palmerston's and Clarendon's view that Bowring's actions at Canton were justified and that Yeh needed a firm lesson. But many members of the Tory Opposition and most of the radicals, including Bowring's former colleagues of the Free Trade and Peace Society movements, such as Cobden and Colonel Thompson, were loud in their denunciation of Bowring and Parkes. Their disapproval was shared by Frederick, though Edgar hastened to his father's support, defending Bowring's action in the *Times*. When the government was defeated after a stormy debate in Parliament and Palmerston called a General Election, Edgar proposed to stand as a candidate himself to uphold his father's honour. He complained that no one in the government had properly defended his father against a charge of deceit (over the expiration of the *Arrow*'s licence) and expressed astonishment that the news of the poisoned bread at Hong Kong had not, at least, momentarily quieted the opposition. Although he was persuaded to give up his plan to stand for Parliament, a pamphlet by 'Lammer Moor' on *Bowring, Cobden and China*, defending Bowring's actions at Canton and deploring his desertion by faithless friends, was either from Edgar's pen or produced with his close co-operation. When the election took place at the end of March, Palmerston's supporters were returned with a large majority, Cobden and many other radicals losing their seats. Even before the election took place, however, Palmerston and Clarendon had decided that Bowring must be replaced as Plenipotentiary and shortly before the election it was announced that the Earl of Elgin would go out to the East to restore peace and conclude a new commercial treaty with China.

Reports of the political storm in England reached Hong Kong at the end of March, to be followed a month later by news of Elgin's appointment as Plenipotentiary and the restriction of Bowring's duties to the governorship of Hong Kong. For Bowring, the suspension of his Plenipotentiary powers was a grievous, if not entirely unexpected, blow, which not even Clarendon's private assurance that he thought Bowring's treatment by Parliament had been most unjust could alleviate. Outwardly he pretended to display a magnanimous attitude to his successor, assuring Elgin of his heartiest co-operation. But he showed himself bitterly resentful over the treatment he had received from his critics in Parliament. As he wrote to Edgar (8 May 1857):

How to thank you for all your devoted kindness, I really know not. How proud I am of your ability and readiness – how pleased with these marks of your affection and devotion – it is indeed hard to find adequate means of expression. But you will have your reward, I doubt not, from many sources ... As to the manner in which I have been spoken of – as I cannot help it – so I must bear it as well as I can ... The way in which I have been personally marked out as the target – is characteristic of the *animus* displayed, for there was no step on which the admiral was not consulted – none which he did not cordially approve and he was the actor, not I, who had no power whatever to control that action if I departed from it – which indeed I never did.

In June, a fresh blow assailed Bowring when he was informed by the Foreign Office that during Elgin's mission to China he was not to leave Hong Kong nor communicate with the mandarins. This was particularly distressing for he had long set his heart on a visit to Japan, where he hoped to obtain a commercial treaty as favourable as the one he had concluded in Siam. Full of indignation at the withdrawal of authority to visit Japan, which had been granted previously by Clarendon, Bowring wrote an angry letter to the Foreign Secretary but decided not to send this and vented his feelings on Edgar (11 June 1857):

> This is the 'unkindest cut of all' and has inflicted a deeper wound on me than anything that has occurred. This is the reward for my success in Siam – where I created a trade that is become enormous employing several thousand vessels. I have been devoting myself for years to the study of the Japanese question ... and now (without a word of explanation) I am superseded. I bent my head resignedly to what was represented to be a Parliamentary necessity in the China affair – but this Japanese wrong is a very cruel and needless injustice – and I assure you is very very hard to bear. My first impulse is to throw up the whole business ... but on reflection – I cannot afford to do what first impulses dictated – and I will bear all – battered and broken as I am – wounded – wearied – wasted – a man whose conduct his masters profess to have approved – but these very masters – these approving masters – give me cups of bitterness and gall to drink.

In the depths of his self-pity and disappointment Bowring looked around for scapegoats to whom to attribute his humiliation. In addition to the officials at the Foreign Office and to some extent, Lord Clarendon, he attached blame for what had happened at Canton to Parkes, confiding to Edgar that he had detected in him 'more than one act of faithlessness'. Parkes for his part was quite willing to leave Hong Kong, informing a friend that 'little else but a sycophant's part' would now satisfy Bowring and that he was not prepared to play. Early in July, however, soon after Elgin's arrival at Hong Kong, a new target for Bowring's spleen and resentment presented himself. This was the writer, George Borrow, whose book *The Romany Rye* was published in England shortly before the attack on Canton.

Bowring had first met Borrow at Norwich in 1821. Ten years later they had collaborated over *Songs of Scandinavia*, the volume of verse translations which, to Borrow's great disappointment, was never published, partly owing to the lack of subscribers but mainly because Bowring, who had published an article on Danish verse in one of the reviews, had lost interest after appointment to his various financial and commercial missions. Bowring and Borrow had kept in touch, however, Bowring providing Borrow with letters of introduction to important people during Borrow's foreign tours on behalf of the Bible Society; and Borrow had become friendly with Bowring's family, professing a great admiration for Bowring's wife. In 1851, when Bowring was at Canton and, as he told Edgar, 'expecting one day to find Borrow entering the Consulate', *Lavengro* had been published. Bowring gave it a cool reception. 'Have you read George Borrow's *Lavengro*?' he wrote to Frederick, 'there are some sketches of character which are very good... but Borrow breaks out into fierce intolerance where the Catholics are concerned – though he knows better. It is less of an honest autobiography than I anticipated from him and far less interesting than he might have made it' (1 May 1851). Frederick, whose anti-Catholic views were as strong as Borrow's, by no means disliked the book. 'I have been much entertained with it', he informed his father. 'What he says is more palatable here than it would be to you. The hatred to the Roman Church and above all to the Jesuits is daily and hourly increasing' (14 December 1851). When *Lavengro*'s successor, *The Romany Rye*, was published in 1857, however, with its full-blooded attack on 'the Old Radical' who 'would do any dirty act which would get him a place', even Frederick was unable to defend it. 'A fellow who unites in himself the bankrupt trader, the broken author or rather book-maker and the laughed-down single-speech spouter of the House of Commons', jeered Borrow, 'may look forward, always supposing he has been a foaming Radical, to the Government of an important colony'. This attack, coming on top of all the other criticisms which were falling

100

on him, roused Bowring to fury. 'I have been reading George Borrow's most mendacious libels in *Romany Rye*', he wrote to Edgar, 'I hunted down *Lavengro* – I cheated him of an appointment and secured it for myself – and then the way in which he has introduced my family (even your mother and sisters) is one of the most impertinent pieces of low rascality I have ever met with. He has carried into the literary field the spirit which other ancient allies have brought into the political – was ever a man pelted from all sides as I have been? I hope I shall survive it all' (24 July 1857).

Much of what Borrow wrote about 'the Old Radical' was concerned with Bowring's pretensions to be a universal linguist, a reputation obtained, according to Borrow, by passing off the translations of 'friendless young men as his own'. Research by various European and American scholars earlier this century revealed that Bowring's reputation as a 'polyglot' was considerably exaggerated. This was indeed suspected at the time and, on the whole, good-humouredly parodied by Bowring's contemporaries in the literary world, long before Borrow's book appeared. Thomas Hood's witty lines about 'Bowring, man of many tongues' and *Fraser's Magazine*'s crueller skit on 'Tydus – Pooh – Pooh (Our Man of Genius) Translator of the Poetry of the Sandwich Isles' are two examples from the period. (*Fraser's* objected more to the 'dirty sycophancy' of Bowring's introductory dedications than to the verses themselves.) It was an age of literary hoaxes and spurious claims and the unacknowledged lifting of other people's writings. Bowring himself suffered from literary piracy as well as practising it when it suited his convenience. In spite of the methods he sometimes employed, the absurd lists of his linguistic attainments (sometimes produced for political purposes) and his very limited knowledge of the languages of Eastern Europe and elsewhere, he had, in fact, real talents both as a linguist and a versifier. Hard-headed contemporaries such as Palmerston and, indeed, Bentham appreciated the former, while even literary giants such as Goethe and Sir Walter Scott paid tribute to the latter.

Borrow's accusation that Bowring had cheated him out of a consular appointment in China by pretending to a parliamentary committee that Borrow's version of a Manchu New Testament was his own work, had little foundation. Bowring's appointment in 1848 had been obtained in circumstances which had nothing to do with his supposed knowledge of Chinese, though he may indeed have given the parliamentary committee on China, of which he was a member, the impression that he was able to understand the language. What provoked Bowring's fury most of all was the scorn poured by Borrow on the religious changes in Bowring's family, a scorn generated by Borrow's hatred of Bowring and his equally strong hatred of the Roman Catholic Church and its High Church imitators within the Established Church. Thus in a chapter preceding the attack on 'the Old Radical', entitled 'Pseudo-Radicals', the situation Maria, Bowring's daughter, found herself in as an unmarriable spinster, attracted to Miss Sellon's 'Sisters of Mercy', was cruelly held up to mockery. A few pages later, both Bowring himself and his wife were savagely caricatured because, according to Borrow, they had attacked him over similarities in *Lavengro* between the dupes of the Catholic priests and the conversions to 'Romanism' within Bowring's family. There is no evidence that Bowring, facing personal disasters from every direction, took any action against that 'coarse liar George Borrow' (1 August 1857), but Borrow's book may have been the last straw which brought him to his bed with a serious attack of fever at the end of July. Moreover Bowring's unfortunate wife (about whom we hear too little in these years) was 'suffering from carbuncles covering her body, destroying her rest, breaking down what there was of strength in her poor frame' (24 July 1857) was still experiencing the adverse effects of the arsenic attack and was moreover finding the stifling heat of Hong Kong increasingly unendurable.

During his last years at Hong Kong misfortunes political and personal continued to heap themselves on Bowring. Elgin, who thought him 'as everybody knows . . . a most dangerous person', avoided him as much as possible. There were endless disputes with the colonial officials and the merchants and most of Bowring's well-intentioned and usually liberal reforms were never successfully put into effect. The disciple of Bentham found it impossible 'practically to Benthamize'. The 'Bowring Praya' [seawall] was never constructed in his time as governor, plans for a civilian hospital, an improved water supply and a new jail were delayed by what Bowring called 'the eminently selfish resistance of the merchants'. 'Hong Kong is always connected to some fatal pestilence, some doubtful war, or some discreditable internal quarrel', complained *The Times* on the 15th March 1850, 'it would be better to send out some sensible man with power to mediate and authority to judge. A man of tact and firmness would settle the

102

matter in a week'. Meanwhile the outbreak of the Indian Mutiny – which was an anxious time for Bowring and his family with their newly married member, Lewin, back in Bengal – prevented Elgin from mounting a naval expedition to China. It was not until December 1857, over a year after Bowring's attack, that Canton was successfully assaulted and the intrepid Chinese Commissioner taken prisoner. When Bowring visited the city which had defied him he found the Chinese as hostile as ever and the danger of attack on foreigners almost as great as before. In July 1858 trouble again broke out at Hong Kong when thousands of Chinese whose families on the mainland were threatened with reprisals fled from the colony, leaving European residents without their household servants. In this predicament reports of a new treaty signed in June between Elgin and the French Plenipotentiary on one side and two Chinese Imperial commissioners on the other at Tientsin, after a naval demonstration at the mouth of the Peiho, came as a great relief to the inhabitants of Hong Kong and they waited impatiently for the return of Elgin's forces to the south. Elgin, however, set off to Japan on the official visit which Bowring had been forced to abandon and the Europeans at Hong Kong and Canton were left to fend for themselves with their limited resources.

By that date Bowring's wife had left the colony with Edith on her way to England, broken down in health and grief-stricken by further family misfortunes. In January news had arrived of the death of Edgar's wife, Sophia, in childbirth. (Edgar married her cousin, Ellen Cubitt, somewhat to his father's surprise.) This was followed almost immediately by the death from fever of Bowring's son Charles at the Jesuit seminary in Rome where he had been since 1855. He had been ordained a priest only shortly before his death. Bowring wrote to Edgar (6 February 1858):

The mail has overwhelmed us in grief and woe for which we were little prepared. We heard of Charles's illness direct in a P.S. to one of his letters – his last letter – and indirectly we had been told he was better – and now comes the miserable and mournful reality not from Rome but first addressed in a letter dated Exeter . . . I wish we could obtain his MSS. and his mementoes which do not belong to the Society. I am most anxious of hearing particulars of his pursuits, his illness and death. Your poor mother has been terribly shaken by this misery – but we think of his purity – his intellectual and moral qualities.

To Frederick, too, Bowring wrote of Charles's death. With this son Bowring's relations had become somewhat strained after hearing of Frederick's disapproval of the attack on Canton. 'I am more anxious in your case than that of any person living to remove the impressions you had entertained of my proceedings in China', Bowring had written, 'unfavourable they assuredly were' (25 October 1857). The coolness between them – perhaps enhanced by Frederick's disappointment over the slow progress of his legal career – was now eased by common grief over the death of Charles. As his father wrote in the same letter:

> It is truly a mystery that children in their ripe age and the full strength of intellect . . . should precede their parents whom they ought rather to follow to the grave . . . The family have been left ignorant of everything connected with his illness, his death and his occupations – he told us so little. In fact he seldom wrote – poor dear, beloved lost. Yet the Jesuits in China had been advised of Charles's illness as I have it from a Catholic here. I think this tearing up the social-domestic-filial ties a sad example of the dislocation of what is purist and holiest in our closest relations – but no murmuring can mend it – or indeed bring a drop of additional comfort – if any comfort is to be found for so grievous a sorrow to our hearts.

Almost the day after his wife's departure from Hong Kong, reports reached Bowring of yet another 'undreamt of blow' in the death of his brother Charles at Liverpool from a lung complaint. This loss added still further to the heavy burden of 'domestic affliction and public adversity'. 'I think myself that his nervous system was broken in upon by the illness of Aunt Anne and then shattered by subsequent events', wrote Frederick to Edgar in a note which has survived (3 April 1858). After these disasters and the return of his wife to England, it is not surprising that Bowring, whose own health was enfeebled by overwork, fever and disappointment, should have made plans for his return to Europe. As he wrote to Edgar (27 May 1858):

Hope is blasted, I am growing to be weary – family sorrows and deprivations have followed one another in desperate visitations – and I shall be glad to be called home. The Government ought to do for me what they have done for all my predecessors – they should give me a pension, a baronetcy and a KCB-ship. John has now a fortune which will enable him to comply with any pecuniary conditions of the baronetcy – and he has some claims on the government for his services in Siam. I do not want to pass another summer in the tropics. Three times I have had the Hong Kong fever and age does not give the stamina to bear up against these repeated attacks. Will you consult Granville – Palmerston – Clarendon – Ellice – as to the course I ought to pursue? I will initiate nothing till I know what is best. But you may say I am a shaken and shattered man as regards my bodily frame – tho' I am not aware that my mind is impaired – or that there has been any neglect in public duty.

Few of Frederick's letters have survived from these years – those that have are in rather a poor condition – and there is no record of his feelings about the death of his brother and uncle. But in a letter to his father in March 1858 he gave a frank but no less dutiful opinion of the situation in China:

You know what I think of this Chinese war and there is no good to pain you by discussing it and after all I probably do not know enough of the facts to form any opinion about the origin of this luckless war. But I think you now err by taking too desponding a view of your situation. You surely must have surmised that you were in fact declaring war and that it must be a serious matter in every view. When the first news came, John, Lewin and I were sitting at Larkbear together and I said, 'this is a much more serious matter than you fancy: I should not be surprised if it lead to my father's recall'. I am happy to find my prophesy has as yet proved false and surely you have nothing to do but to watch the progress of events ... I am sorry you flung away as I think the certain cards of safe and gradual progress to make this desperate fling, chiefly because I fear it will prevent justice being done to your really great acts in Siam and administration generally ... For you to resign now would

105

be certain downfall and it could not but enrage Palmerston as much as it would delight the Derbyites. I confess I agree most with Disraeli and the Tory view of foreign politics, though I don't have especially any. (7 March 1858)

It was not yet the end of family misfortunes. In October 1858 reports reached Bowring that his sick wife, who had obtained shelter with her relations in Taunton, was rapidly getting worse. A month later the tragic news arrived that his wife Maria was dying – in fact she passed away on 27 September 1858. 'She suffered much, but died calmly and resignedly' wrote her brother-in-law, Thomas Ward, in his diary. It is difficult to assess the effect of this calamity on Bowring, for even in his letters to Edgar praising his dead wife's virtues, he found space to discuss mundane details about Chinese trade and to express his own mortification at having lost the opportunity to conclude a new treaty with China (13 November 1858). But it is likely that the death of his wife thousands of miles away greatly increased his feeling of isolation and self-pity, though these sentiments do not seem to have been shared by much sense of responsibility for the sufferings which had brought about her decease.

Discredited, wracked by frequent attacks of fever, lonely, though he still had two daughters and his son John with him (for Emily had now arrived at Hong Kong), Bowring began to wonder whether he was not about to follow his wife 'to the dark passages of death'. Even at this period, however, something of his restless spirit remained. At the end of November 1858 he was advised by his doctors to get away from Hong Kong and set out on a six week tour of the Philippine Islands, which were still at this date under Spanish rule. There, amid fresh surroundings and away from the bickerings of his colonial officials and the hostility of the merchants, his health somewhat recovered and he was soon dashing around with his accustomed energy. 'I have been received here as to the court of a King', he wrote to Edgar from Manila, 'large bodies of troops to welcome my landing – a carriage and four to drive me to the palace . . . I am getting young again with all the reminiscences of Spain in my memory' (13 December 1858). By the time he returned to Hong Kong in January 1859 his zeal for spreading the benefits of commercial prosperity to backward Asian lands had fully revived. It is not surprising therefore, that, in spite of his constantly expressed desire to return home, he read with indignation a despatch from the Tory Foreign Secretary, Lord Malmesbury, informing him that the government had appointed Lord Elgin's brother, Frederick Bruce, as First Minister Plenipotentiary accredited to the Imperial Court and Chief Superintendent of Trade, and he himself was expressly forbidden to enter into any communication with the Chinese authorities between the conclusion of Elgin's special mission to Japan and the arrival of Bruce. Even the news that his request for a pension had been granted and that the Colonial Office would allow him to delegate his colonial duties to the Lieutenant-Governor as soon as Bruce arrived at Hong Kong failed to console him. 'I shall hand on the colony in a state of the highest prosperity', he assured Clarendon, 'but I return to England a shattered old man'. The peremptory tone of Malmesbury's despatch provoked an angry reaction from Edgar, who protested to Hammond at the Foreign Office about the way in which his father had been superseded 'and a moment chosen for sending him this news when he has just been struck down by the most terrible calamity that can befall a man . . . the course adopted is eminently calculated to cause pain not only to himself but to all his family'.

Back at Government House, Bowring once again succumbed to an attack of fever and was still on his sickbed, (where he devoted his time to preparing a book on the Philippines), when Elgin arrived back at Hong Kong from Japan and Shanghai. Bowring was greatly offended by Elgin's off hand treatment of himself. 'I have seen enough of him to know how willing he is to efface all claims but his own and to use his influence very unjustly and very selfishly', he complained to Edgar (3 March 1859). He was not, however, obliged to endure the Plenipotentiary's contemptuous indifference for long, for early in March Elgin set out abruptly for Europe, leaving the remaining problems of China to be settled by his brother after his arrival in the East.

After the return of Elgin to Europe, Bowring was once again, for a brief period, left in sole authority. But this was little consolation to him as Lord Malmesbury did not even consult him about matters, such as the operation of the Shanghai Customs Inspectorate system, with which he had been closely connected. Even now, however, he was unable to await his successor in idleness. Early in April he paid a final visit to Canton, officially in order to discuss emigration problems with the consul. But there is no doubt he was also anxious to take a final look at the city which had been the scene of his greatest humiliations. 'I took the girls to see the ruined and blank site of the factories', Bowring, who had brought Maria and Emily with him, wrote to Edgar, 'it is a sad spectacle – the gardens look as if they had been ploughed up – with deep holes and ditches – heaps of broken bricks and dust. The east quarter of the city is quite destroyed' (8 April 1859).

It was Emily who provided Bowring with his final shock before his departure from China. Now, on the eve of her father's retirement, she announced her intention of remaining in the East and joining a Catholic religious order engaged in missionary work amongst the native children. Bowring was very upset by Emily's decision and spoke of clandestine attempts by Catholic priests to get her into a convent. 'Emily's obstinacy says it is the Will of God she should devote herself to the salvation of the souls of these heathen little ones', he wrote to Edgar. 'All remonstrances have hitherto been in vain. She is stern and unmanageable' (3 March 1859). 'I cannot understand the light heartedness and complacency with which she contemplates the separation which to me is death as she is lost for ever to all of us on earth ... I did not want another blow for my prostration ... one after another having fallen so heavily' (25 May 1859). None of his appeals, however, could move Emily from her determination to remain in China and he was finally forced to leave her behind, well aware he would never see his youngest daughter again. Emily was to die in a convent in China in 1870. Some lines of verse addressed to 'E.B.' and published after Bowring's death are probably for her.

At the end of April Bruce arrived at Hong Kong and Bowring was free to leave the colony. On 3 May he formally handed over his duties and, accompanied by Maria, set out on the journey to England. Although he had been governor of Hong Kong longer than his predecessors, he was so unpopular that few Europeans paid much attention to his departure. Some of the Chinese, however, presented him with gifts and addresses of appreciation for the reforms he had tried to introduce. Even now his misfortunes were not at an end. As the *Alma*, the ship on which Maria and he were sailing from Ceylon to Egypt, was crossing the Red Sea it struck a submerged coral reef and all those on board narrowly escaped drowning. Maria, so her brother Lewin later wrote, 'landed on a coral reef in nothing but her night gown'. (Death at sea, like death in childbirth, was a hazard of the age – Bowring's early friend, Blaquiere, and Lant Carpenter were both drowned.) Eventually, after three days of privation, the passengers were picked up by another British ship and conveyed back to Aden to await fresh transportation. The incident provided Bowring with material for an article in *Once a Week*, but at the time it must have been an unpleasant experience and he lost many of his papers and personal possessions.

7

The Old Radical when Old

When Bowring returned from the Far East in 1859, he was 67 years old, weakened in health and overwhelmed by public and personal disasters. It might have been expected, therefore, that he would seek consolation away from constant attack and the intrigues of ungrateful politicians. Yet nothing is more characteristic of the man than his refusal to consider his political career at an end. As he made his way back to England, his mind was already full of active plans for the future. 'My improved health has altered my thoughts and purposes', he wrote to Edgar from the ship. 'What I should best like would be a seat in Parliament with some official position in the government. If this cannot be, I dare say my old friends, if in power ... would give me some diplomatic appointment – idle I cannot be' (26 May 1859).

It is not easy to trace Bowring's attempts to re-enter public life, for the long series of letters to his family, which are so useful during his administration in China, do not cover these last years. But it is clear that he neglected no opportunity to vindicate his reputation and to pick up the threads of his former career as a radical politician. After the Whig return to office, he sought an increase to his pension, for which he was eventually given an additional special allowance. He also sought the grant of a KCB – the order of Knight Commander of the Bath – but, in spite of an application by Ellice on Bowring's behalf, his former patrons were unwilling to stir up political differences by granting him the honour. With the help of Edgar, he made efforts to justify the role he had played in China, particularly after the renewal of hostilities in northern China in 1860 and Elgin's return to the East, publishing *A Brief Statement of the Public Services of Sir John Bowring*. He toured the industrial cities of the midlands and north, explaining to local commercial associations the motives which

110

Sir John Bowring, 1866 Album of 'Men of Eminence'

had caused him to act as he did. 'No man was ever a more ardent lover of peace than I', he protested, 'but with barbarians – ay, and sometimes with civilised nations, the words of peace are uttered in vain'. He tried, without success, to renew his friendship with Colonel Thompson and Cobden – Cobden cutting him to his face in the Athenaeum club. In particular, he tried to secure a seat in Parliament for the city of his birth.

Bowring's hopes of becoming an MP for Exeter seemed at first not without some foundation, for although the city had formerly returned one Tory and one Liberal member, Palmerston's government had introduced a new reform bill that was expected to place the representation in the hands of an increased electorate, which would return two Liberal members to Parliament. Moreover, the leader of the Exeter reformers, Thomas Latimer, editor of the *Western Times*, was an old acquaintance of Bowring's dating back to the days with Bentham, when Latimer had been secretary of a short-lived London Gymnastic Society. Like Bowring himself, he was a zealous free trader, supporter of Palmerston and a determined opponent of the Anglican Church, in particular of Bishop Phillpotts. During the early months of 1860, therefore, Bowring devoted much attention to Exeter politics, assisting Latimer in the formation of a local Liberal Registration Society, with a low subscription to encourage working-class membership, and inaugurating a Free Discussion Society, with himself as president, to disseminate such radical reforms as the ballot and universal state education. Meanwhile Latimer started a campaign in the *Western Times*, drawing attention to Bowring's public services in China and making much of his Exeter origins, to which the Tory *Exeter and Plymouth Gazette* replied by publishing all the unsavoury gossip it could discover about Bowring's conduct in China and elsewhere. All this activity, however, came to nothing for in July 1860 Palmerston's government withdrew its reform bill and the chances of an early revision of the franchise disappeared. Three months later a meeting of the Exeter Liberal electors officially adopted a non-Exonian as their first choice of candidate in a future election. After this Bowring, who realised his chances of winning a seat as second Liberal candidate were slight, withdrew his offer to stand, ostensibly on the grounds that other public duties made it impossible for him to seek election. But it must have been a bitter humiliation to find himself set aside in favour of a Liberal rival.

As the likelihood of a seat in Parliament disappeared, Bowring began to turn his attention to developments on the continent, where he hoped to secure public employment in his old role as commercial investigator. The conclusion of a free trade treaty with France in 1860 made a considerable impression on him and although he publicly described Cobden's success in negotiations as 'beyond all praise', he was extremely jealous that his former free trade colleague had succeeded where he himself had failed. He hurried over to Paris in February 1860 and obtained an unofficial interview with the French Emperor, Napoleon III, which Bowring considered most beneficial to the development of the treaty. Even more momentous, however, were the changes which were taking place in Italy, where the later months of 1860 witnessed the culmination of the long struggle for Italian emancipation from Austrian and Bourbon control. Bowring, remembering his many years of acquaintance with the Italian liberals (and forgetting sentiments he had expressed in different circumstances in China), was greatly excited by these events and eager to meet the heroes of the liberation. Moreover, he hoped to take advantage of the good relations between Great Britain and the new Kingdom of Italy to secure a commercial treaty which would rank as equal to Cobden's achievement in France. Immediately, therefore, after his second marriage (see p. 000 below) Bowring, accompanied by his new wife, set out for the continent and after a few weeks' stay in Paris, crossed the Alps and in December secured an interview with Count Cavour at Turin. The results of the meeting were reported to Lord John Russell, now Foreign Secretary. Bowring described his dinner with Cavour, 'a very old personal acquaintance of mine', dwelt on the enthusiasm of the Italian government for a commercial treaty and emphasised his own particular suitability for the appointment of negotiator, for which 'my acquaintance with the language of the country and so many of the leading statesmen would give me some advantage'. In later years Bowring gave the impression that he had been expressly sent by Palmerston and Russell on a commercial mission to the new Italian kingdom, but it is clear that the initiative for an appointment came from himself. Whatever his opinion of Bowring's conduct in China, Russell was not averse to making use of his experience as a commercial agent, especially when his services were freely offered.

Bowring's investigation, however, was not to be completed for early in 1861 he was prostrated by an attack of fever which came upon him at Rome, shortly after an interview with the Pope. (One wonders whether Bowring visited the grave of his son Charles.) By the middle of February he was sufficiently recovered to send Russell a letter accepting his semi-official appointment, but soon afterwards he suffered a relapse and according to his wife 'for months ... hovered between life and death'. Eventually he was well enough to get down to his duties. In June, however, Cavour died whilst Bowring was at Leghorn and in the disorganisation following his death, all hopes of a commercial agreement came to an end. Faced with no prospects of carrying out his plans, Bowring left Italy for Malta. But at Valetta in the intense summer heat he was again taken seriously ill and was obliged to return to England. There, in the quiet of Larkbear (where he had taken up residence on his return from China), his health slowly recovered, though even in November he was not well enough to take the chair at a Unitarian conference in Exeter. By early 1862 he was almost himself and was soon busy writing letters to the press setting forth his views on the American Civil War in which, in spite of his abhorrence of slavery, his sympathies lay with the separatist claims of the South. That summer he suffered an attack of gout, which he treated by taking the waters at Bad Homburg in Germany. But his general health continued to improve and in the autumn he was able to resume his normal round of engagements. Never again, until his final illness, was he to come so near to death as he had done in 1861.

On his return to Exeter from China, Bowring resumed an active role in Unitarian affairs, once again attending George's Meeting, which had much declined in prestige since his youth. It was, however, at Lewin's Mead Unitarian chapel in Bristol that he was married in November 1860 to Deborah Castle, the 44-years-old daughter of the late Thomas Castle, a prominent Clifton Unitarian. Bowring had had associations with Lewin's Mead chapel since Lant Carpenter's days as minister and had probably been acquainted with the Castle family before his years in China. The marriage was performed by R P Aspland, son of the former minister of the Gravel Pit Congregation at Hackney.

Their father's second marriage came as a great shock to Bowring's family, only one of whom, Maria, attended the ceremony. A letter from Frederick to Lewin in India, describing their reactions, has fortunately survived (2 December 1860):

Shall you have anticipated the deuce's own shindy caused by my father's second marriage? Married he and Miss Castle were to be and married they were ... and are now finishing their honeymoon in Paris. I must tell my own story in my own way. Edith was excessively afflicted and annoyed and stupified by the news of father's intended marriage and is quite determined not to live with them. She and father had a very painful interview just before the wedding and parted mutually dissatisfied. I think my father felt more than he betrayed and as he was wont to count on Edith's judgement and affection, it must have been very painful to him to see how much this step had alienated her from him. Next I put my foot in it though innocently (fancy an innocent lawyer aged 38!). I could not indeed bring myself to

114

write very congratulatory letters but I did write civilly and politely to Miss Castle and as far as I am concerned resolved not to make bad worse. But seeing how matters stood and how hard it was on my sisters to be so completely dependent on a father married to a wife not much older than themselves, I determined to write and wrote to him saying I thought (and I believed my brothers would think with me) that he ought to increase my sisters' allowances and allow them to live at Larkbear and if they pleased – and to this my father readily responded and said he would do so. A few days after comes a letter from Maria complaining of my interference wishing to banish them to Larkbear and passionately rejecting all increase of allowance, so my father seems to have considered the whole at an end and told Edith he would offer her a home in his own house but would do nothing further at present. And in fact he has I am told (for I refused to be trustee) settled his fortune on his wife for her life. It is easy enough to see that in case of my father's death my sisters' interests would be postponed during the life of a woman not much older and a much better life than themselves. I say nothing of us men, as we do not care about it and indeed the only anxiety I have felt is that my father would provide for our sisters. But for Maria's foolish interference I have no doubt this would have taken place. Edith has her friend Miss Gallard but Maria has no such personal friend so I can understand the latter's present wish to live with my father and his second wife but I much doubt if she will like it. I don't think there is likely to be much cordiality between us and the new Lady Bowring. We have not heard from you or John yet so cannot tell what view you take but I believe I may claim the credit of not having written to you in an exaggerated way, annoyed as I was.

In a final sentence Frederick described his father playing at Larkbear with his two grandchildren, Edgar's sons: 'I left it to the Governor of Hong Kong to teach them the use of the longbow'. One of these small boys, Edgar Frances ('Edgarino') was to become an Anglican clergyman, Rural Dean of Godalming and Honorary Canon of Winchester. The other, Algernon Cunliffe, rose to be a high official of the Roman Catholic Church. Both boys, as well as a younger brother, were educated at Wellington and Cambridge.

Little is known about the later fortunes of Bowring's two unmarried daughters. In spite of their accomplishments they faced the predicament of many Victorian spinsters of their class: no regular occupation outside a family circle which, with their mother's death and their father's remarriage, was for them steadily diminishing. Like her sister Emily, Maria had sought fulfilment in a religious community at variance with the rationalist religious doctrines of her upbringing. But family disapproval and public ridicule, extending even to the pages of a work of fiction, brought to an end this attempt to escape from her melancholy situation.

The second Lady Bowring proved to be an energetic companion to Bowring in his later years, accompanying him on his journeys abroad, nursing him during his illnesses, encouraging his political and religious activities and, after his death, publishing a collection of his sacred verses, prefaced by a brief memoir. A good public speaker and an active participant in many local organisations, she lived until 1902. In their early married days Bowring and his second wife dwelt at Larkbear, but after John's return to England they moved into a new house named 'Claremont' at a short distance from the old family home, (engraved notepaper, headed 'Claremont' and bearing Bowring's coat of arms, a lion rampant surmounted by a scroll inscribed 'Onward', now made its appearance).

It was probably with his second wife's encouragement that soon after his marriage Bowring, whose Unitarian zeal was rather less in evidence during his years of authority in China, published an attack on the Trinitarian doctrine of the Athanasian Creed, under the initials LLD. The article showed that he had lost none of his literary powers but must have given pain to his Anglican and Roman Catholic sons and daughters. He followed this with enthusiastic reviews of Renan's *Vie de Jésus*, but was careful not to court charges of atheism by making an English translation of the work. As a Unitarian he was particularly interested in the religious implications of Darwin's and Lyall's biological and geological theories. He became friendly with William Pengelly, a local geologist and fellow member of the Devonshire Association, a man familiar with the abundant geological evidence near the Dorset and Devon coasts.

During his retirement Bowring kept up a considerable correspondence on a large variety of topics. In June 1866 he gave some useful advice to one of his earliest acquaintances whom he had known since she was a child, Mary Carpenter, Lant Carpenter's daughter, who had been born at Exeter. By this time she was well known for her philanthropic and educational work and was preparing to visit India, where she planned to establish schools and training colleges for Hindu women. Bowring, whose personal knowledge of India was limited to his visit to Bengal and correspondence with his son Lewin on the 10 June 1866, warned her of the difficulties she could encounter:

> If matters are what they were when I visited Calcutta, I hope you will see your way very clearly before you venture on a field where much discouragement and disappointment may await you – when the difficulties of the language – the inaccessibleness of the *Zenanas* – and the repugnance of the high classes of women to intercourse with Christian ladies may be a great barrier to you – and where the influences of caste still create many disagreeable positions . . . I shall be anxious about your health – particularly in the hot season and can only hope and pray that all may be well with you.

Although Mary Carpenter visited India four times, few of her educational schemes got off the ground successfully, mainly for the reasons Bowring had mentioned, and she did, indeed, suffer some ill health in India. The letter provides a good example of Bowring's lifelong ability, except when stirred by strong passion or personal prejudice or the desire to impress, to provide useful and practical information about circumstances in various parts of the world.

After their return from the East, both Bowring and, later, his son John were appointed JPs. They regularly took part in magisterial duties at Exeter Castle, sometimes sitting together on the Bench. Since his days with Bentham and his practical experience of a cell at Boulogne, Bowring had taken a keen interest in penal reforms and he had frequently visited prisons on the continent and in the East. As JP and a Deputy Lord Lieutenant for Devon, he devoted much time to this subject, advocating the substitution of productive prison labour for such antiquated punishments as the treadmill, which was still used in Devon jails. In 1865 he published *Remunerative Prison Labour as an Instrument for Promoting the Reformation and Diminishing the Cost of Offenders*, based on an address he had delivered

117

to the county magistrates at Quarter Sessions. Later he made a tour of the nation's jails, describing his impression of prison conditions to the British Association. As a JP attending Quarter Sessions, Bowring also advocated a degree of financial and administrative reform, similar to the measures recommended for central government by the Public Accounts Committee, of which he had been secretary nearly forty years earlier. As at Hong Kong, however, Bowring's penal and financial reform proposals, far-seeing as many of them were, soon ran into opposition, many of the county squires who dominated the Bench and Quarter Sessions having, like the Hong Kong merchants, a vested interest in the *status quo* and looking askance at Bowring's radical opinions and political reputation.

His concern with prison labour and administrative reform prompted Bowring in 1865 to reopen correspondence with his fellow disciple of Bentham, Edwin Chadwick. 'Here in my self-solitude', he wrote, 'I am endeavouring in my old age practically to Benthamize. I have been mooting the question of productive labour among prisoners and paupers – one does not make much progress among county justices and parsons who find punishment an easier task than the reform of offenders'. Chadwick's friendly reply encouraged Bowring to continue the correspondence, which developed into an exchange of reminiscences particularly about the last days of Bentham. Bowring, who had not formerly troubled much over the disposal of the philosopher's relics, now declared himself concerned about the condition of Bentham's effigy, which had been handed over to London University by Southwood Smith in 1860. In 1866 he visited the college, finding the case, so he informed Chadwick, 'in a most unsatisfactory state – neglected – and I fear moths had attacked the garments – Could you call on Mr Atkinson and see Mr Grote – and advise what measures should be adopted? – I seldom visit town'. No steps were taken, however, to deal with Bentham's relics until after Bowring's death when Chadwick tried in vain to obtain from Bowring's son John such papers referring to Bentham as were still in the Bowring family's possession. (The bulk of Bentham's manuscripts had been passed over to London University at the time of Bowring's departure for China.)

During his years of retirement, Bowring was again able to devote time to literary activities. He had always been prolific and now hymns, verse translations and magazine articles flowed regularly from his pen. A projected book on China, on the lines of his volumes on Siam and the Philippines, never appeared, but he contributed articles on Chinese customs to the periodicals of the day. In 1868 he published a translation of a Chinese story, *The Flowery Scroll*, containing copious footnotes on Chinese culture and seemingly translated by the author direct from the Chinese. But, in fact, both this work and a translation of the verse of the Magyar poet, Alexander Petofi, which he published two years earlier, were based on recent German versions which Bowring, true to the habits of former years, had used without acknowledgement. During his months of convalescence in 1861 Bowring had started to write an autobiography but got little further than his childhood days at Exeter and brief notes on international celebrities he had known. The memories of his youth, however, aroused in him an interest in the city of his birth and he began to devote time to the history and antiquities of Exeter, producing a paper for the Devonshire Association on the Devon dialects. He also wrote two articles on Exeter 'Sixty Years Ago' for Dickens's *All the Year Round*, illustrating the differences between the thriving port of his youth and the somewhat decayed cathedral city of his old age.

Literary and antiquarian pursuits, however engaging, were no substitute to Bowring for practical political activity. The extension of the suffrage by the 1867 Reform Act increased the chances for Exeter Liberals to secure two seats in Parliament (one Liberal member having been elected in 1865) and Bowring was determined to make the most of the situation. He himself, at 75, was too old and infirm for duties at Westminster, though he still frequently spoke on political platforms and it was through his influence that his son, John, was adopted as one of the Liberal candidates. After his return from China, John, now a wealthy man, married Isabella Toulmin and took up residence at Larkbear, which he completely rebuilt. (When his first wife died, John, like his two brothers, remarried and raised a large family.) Before the first election under the new franchise took place in 1868, however, John withdrew his candidature in favour of Edgar, who had retired from the Board of Trade on a pension in 1863, after the abolition of his post of Registrar. John, who was not a good speaker and was more interested in natural history than politics – he later presented a magnificent collection of Coleoptera (beetles) to the British Museum – was persuaded by his father to make way for Edgar after the politically experienced but younger

119

brother had failed to secure the Liberal nomination at Bristol. (Frederick had been offered the opportunity at Exeter, as an older brother, but, not surprisingly, had turned it down.) The decision was undoubtedly a sound one as Edgar's abilities resembled his father's more than those of any of his brothers. He had published several foreign verse translations from the German, composed a metrical version of the psalms and written pamphlets on economic matters, including the adoption of decimal coinage. He had risen energetically to the assistance of his father during the Shanghai customs duties dispute and supported him during the *Arrow* political crisis of 1857. He was also familiar with Whitehall and Westminster. In the actual election campaign Bowring himself took little part, probably to avoid embarrassing Edgar by his presence on the platform. But this did not prevent the local Tory press launching personal attacks on him as well as against his son, including the display of a series of political posters which drew the attention of the electors to the most embarrassing incidents in Bowring's career, such as the Greek loan scandals of more than 40 years earlier. The first of the posters, 'respectfully dedicated – without permission – to Edgar Bowring Esq', showed the candidate's father carrying a large Greek pie. In another political squib 'Young Edgar Sly-Boots (son of Sir Opium Sly-Boots)' was portrayed as being as great a place-seeker as his father. In spite of the virulence of the Tory campaign, which equalled the hostility of Bowring's opponents at Blackburn and Bolton in earlier elections, both Liberal candidates were elected, Edgar by a small majority in the last hour of the poll when many working men recorded their votes. The election was successful for the Liberal party as a whole, for they were returned to office with a majority of 112 and Gladstone became Prime Minister. Edgar lost his seat when the Tories came back to power in the 1874 election and never re-entered Parliament.

During his years of retirement Bowring had found an outlet for his free trade zeal in acting as commercial agent on behalf both of the government of Siam and of the Hawaian Islands, with which he had first established contact during his period as Superintendent of Trade in China. For these duties, which involved him in a large correspondence with the London ambassadors and consular officials of the countries concerned, he received several high-sounding decorations, such as the Grand Cordon of Kamehameha, though he was not allowed to wear them on ceremonial occasions in England. As

The Times drily pointed out, honours such as the insignia of the White Elephant of Siam had little meaning, though they helped to gratify Bowring's vanity and gave, perhaps, some compensation for his failure to obtain a KCB. When, in his old age, he started somewhat emotionally to piece together his 'Recollections', he reminded his readers – and perhaps himself – that he went to China 'as a representative of the Queen accredited not to Peking alone but to Japan, Siam, China and Korea – I believe to a greater number of human beings (indeed, no less than a third of the human race) than an individual has been accredited to before'. But as the Exeter *Western Times* pointed out, there was a conflict between his wish to be regarded as a leader of the democratic party and 'his willingness to accept an order of nobility from the hand of any potentate either in Christian or in pagan lands'.

The return of Lord Clarendon to the Foreign Office during the later 1860s prompted Bowring to make one more attempt to secure the long-desired KCB. He had seen little of his 'dear Villiers' in recent years but he remained anxious to add to his many foreign honours the award which would vindicate his reputation in diplomatic circles. It must have been a great disappointment to Bowring, therefore, when Clarendon's promise of assistance was once more not followed by any concrete results and his ability to gratify his old colleague was lost for ever by his death in 1870. Neither Palmerston nor Bowring's patron Ellice were any longer alive. Bowring, however, was not to be easily deterred and in 1871 he wrote direct to Gladstone, setting forth his case in detail and listing the multitude of honours he had received from numerous European and Asian governments. 'At my advanced age', he wrote, 'the susceptibility may be forgiven which feels that my position implies I have discharged my public duties less worthily than those who preceeded me'. Gladstone referred Bowring's letter to Lord Granville (the son of Bowring's old associate in France), who might have been expected to look sympathetically into the affair, in view of his former acquaintance with Bowring's family. Granville, however, had never approved of Bowring's policy in China and he pointed out that the claims were 'of an ancient date and somewhat doubtful'. He also informed the Prime Minister that Edgar Bowring was seeking the same award for his services to the Great Exhibition. Consequently Gladstone wrote to Bowring's family refusing his request for a decoration. Either he

121

or Granville must have informed Edgar, who was under attack in Parliament on account of his pension from the Board of Trade, that a KCB for his Exhibition services was out of the question. Edgar was later awarded the CB (Companion of the Order of the Bath).

Little is known about family affairs in these years in the absence of much correspondence. In 1871 Lewin, who had been Chief Commissioner of Mysore and Courg, resigned from office and returned to Britain, taking up residence at Torquay where, a zealous Roman Catholic and strong conservative, he took an active part in local affairs. Like John and Edgar, he married twice, becoming father to a large family. Two of his sons later served in India where one of them, Captain John Bowring, was murdered by a sepoy in 1904. Thus by 1872 all the surviving members of Bowring's family were back in England and all his sons, except Frederick, who was to remain a bachelor, had married and provided Bowring with grandchildren. In October 1872 Bowring celebrated his eightieth birthday at Claremont in the company of his family. A week later he appeared at a political meeting organised by Edgar and the other Exeter MP. Edgar had recently spoken in Parliament in the debate in which the Ballot Act became law. During these last years, Bowring had frequently suffered some ill health, though his letters and photographs of him in his seventies suggest that he remained in full possession of his faculties. Early in November, however, he was taken ill with gout and on 23 November he died at Claremont, only a short distance from where he had been born.

Bowring was buried in the Exeter New Cemetery after a brief funeral service at George's Meeting, attended by all his family and a large number of local worthies. His gravestone bore the opening lines of one of his best-known hymns: 'In the Cross of Christ I Glory'. More appropriate, perhaps, are some farewell lines he had written many years earlier and which were published in Lady Bowring's *Memorial Volume of Sacred Poetry*:

> My wife, my children, when death's hour is come
> Dry every every gushing tear, I pray
> And rather smile that I am welcomed home
> And to a better country make my way.

Most obituaries contained a brief summary of his life prepared by

122

Bowring himself and accompanied by appropriately pious remarks. 'Without ranking with the foremost spirits of the time', wrote the Liberal *Daily Telegraph*, 'he was emphatically a remarkable man and if it was possible to measure the lifework of Jeremy Bentham's favourite pupil, it would be found that Sir John Bowring had done a good deal more than the average amount for 'the Greatest Happiness of the Greatest Number'. Let it be honourably said that his activity was almost always on the side of human progress, that he was enlightened in religious and social respects and that his support was seldom wanted for a good cause . . . Sir John is fresh proof that men may thrive on hard work and die in idleness'. A less sympathetic account in the Tory *Exeter and Plymouth Gazette*, while admitting that he had 'crowded an amazing amount of activity into a lifetime of 80 years', thought that 'he did too much to do it all well' and drew attention to the 'singular fact that not one of his family adopted his religious views. The father was strongly rationalistic: the children belong to the very opposite school of thought'.

Allowing for newspaper exaggeration – for several of his children never embraced Catholicism – the religious changes within Bowring's family merit some consideration. The theory that his offspring were turning against years of regular family worship in the somewhat austere setting of a Unitarian chapel, George's Meeting or the New Gravel Pit, for example, gains some support from Bowring's assurance in his letters to Frederick, and no doubt to his other children, that his liberal principles in matters of religious belief would not allow him to subject his family to doctrinal pressure of any kind. That there were limits to Bowring's liberal sentiments is apparent from his whole career. But the Mr Howard-like pose of 'benevolence' appears to be generally valid in relations with his young family. In the correspondence of Frederick Bowring, Frederick's hostility is directed not against Unitarianism, no doubt to avoid upsetting his parents, for both of whom he expressed strong affection, but against the Roman church and Anglo-Catholicism. The advantages to Frederick of becoming a member of the Established church, probably under the influence of his two Anglican aunts and the staff at Exeter Cathedral, are clear in view of his disadvantageous position as a nonconformist at Trinity College, Cambridge. But these advantages were hardly available to Catholic converts who, by mid-century were attracting as much public hostility as Bowring's co-religionists had done in earlier times when his grandfather was burned in effigy at Exeter. (That Unitarians could themselves display intolerance to those who did not share their views is evident from their role in a largely non-conformist organisation like the British and Foreign School Society.)

To explain, therefore, the influences which persuaded several of Bowring's family to abandon both their rationalist Unitarian upbringing and Low Church Anglicanism and accept either Anglo-Catholicism or the authority of Rome, one needs to consider the coincidence in time of the arrival of Bowring's offspring at mature but impressionable years with the increasing prominence of Anglo-Catholicism and Roman-Catholicism in England, (just as Bowring's own youth had coincided with the wave of radicalism that swept over Europe during the closing stages of the Napoleonic Wars). Also significant is the family's close connection with Exeter. In Bowring's youth Unitarianism in Exeter had been strong, as witnessed by the prestige of George's Meeting in Kenrick's and Lant Carpenter's days. But with the decline of the Devonshire cloth trade local Unitarianism had also declined, though it revived to some extent after Bowring's return from China. On the other hand, High Church Anglicanism was increasing in the Exeter area during the episcopate of the formidable bishop Phillpotts and the influence of Puseyite enthusiasts, such as Priscilla Sellon. Roman Catholicism, however, though established in the city, was not so strong, though it was making steady progress in the country as a whole, especially in mid-century when the Catholic hierarchy was re-established and seminaries such as Stonyhurst were thriving. As many contempories realised, this increase in English Catholicism was due not only to Irish immigration but to a reaction against the religious rationalism and scepticism furthered by the philosophies of Bentham and Mill and the scientific discoveries 'beyond the Christian pale', which so impressed Bowring and other Unitarians. Hostility to this Catholic revival was strong, particularly amongst many Low Church Anglicans and other evangelicals. In the present context this is illustrated not only by Bowring's attacks on 'Romanism', but by the equally strong expressions of hostility by Frederick Bowring, himself an Anglican convert, who was a scholar at Cambridge where, unlike Oxford, opposition both to Tractarian influences and to Catholicism was often strong. How then, in spite of a wide measure of family and social disapproval, can the adher-

124

ence of several members of Bowring's family to these unpopular creeds be explained?

In middle-class Victorian society certain people were particularly likely to be attracted to Anglo-Catholicism and Roman Catholicism. The single woman, with few marriage or career prospects, except as governess or lady-companion or as 'mother's guardian angel', could dedicate her life to the service of a religious community, perhaps as a 'Sister of Mercy', as in Maria's case, or as a Catholic nun, concerned, as in Emily's case, with the welfare of the 'heathen' children of China. Similarly the single young man like Charles, unsuited to the demands of commercial or professional life, uninterested in money-making (as his father observed), unimpressed by the material progress of the age with its optimistic slogans such as the 'Tide of Tendency' and the 'March of Improvement' might prefer the self-sacrifice of a religious community. To these conversions the other members of Bowring's family, including Bowring himself when pushed to the limit, reacted strongly. Frederick in particular opposed the religious changes of Charles, Maria and Emily, seeing their actions as a sign of weakness of mind or even madness. But Frederick's fellow 'Exonian', Lewin, whom his brother would have never accused of weakness, also became a Roman Catholic and in his later years a strong conservative, rejecting both his father's political and religious radicalism. (The irony of his second name, 'Bentham', adhered to him throughout life.) The habits of his authoritarian position in India as a District Commissioner perhaps help to explain Lewin's outlook. Did he, however, like his aunt Lucy and his sister Emily, pass through the Established Church on his way to Rome and was he influenced by his close links with the Exeter family?

There is little to add about the religious sentiments of John and Edgar, though Edgar's religious interests are indicated by his metrical version of the psalms. That he became, like Frederick, a regular member of the Established Church is evident from his comments during the 1867 election when he courted the votes of Exeter Low Churchmen and non-conformists. But in his family, too, one son was to become an influential figure in the Roman Catholic Church. How about the devoted Edith? Did she remain Unitarian during her mother's lifetime and what happened to her faith after the rift with her father, whose reinforced Unitarian zeal displayed itself after his return from China and his second marriage?

After Bowring's death his papers went to his eldest son, John, who moved away from Exeter to the Windsor area. It was Lewin, however, who edited his father's reminiscences, publishing in 1877 *The Autobiographical Recollections of Sir John Bowring*, with a reproduction of the d'Angers medallion on the front of the book. Lewin made no attempt to produce a full biography, though he found room to express his own lack of sympathy with his father's views and considered it 'a subject of regret that a better cause of quarrel with the Chinese was not found than the *Arrow* Affair'. Years earlier Frederick had urged his father to write his autobiography, 'which to all of us would be a precious possession as a genuine memorial to one whom we all love and honour and whom I have no doubt many generations of our race (should there be such) will be proud to have as an ancestor' (10 May 1854). The *Autobiographical Recollections*, however, were not generally well received, partly for their subject's 'conceit', partly for the *ex tempore* presentation of the book, and were adversely quoted against Bowring in attacks on his reputation in succeeding years. For although Bowring was dead, he was not allowed to rest in peace. Even before his demise, Cobden's biographer, John Morley, had declared that 'agents like Bowring should not only be recalled but should be formally disgraced and explicitly punished'. In 1879 Justin McCarthy produced his *History of Our Own Times*, which contained a verbose condemnation of the conduct of Bowring, who 'set up early for a sort of great man' and whose 'eager self-conceit would not allow him to resist the temptation to display himself as . . . a master spirit of the order of Clive and Warren Hastings, bidding the English be of good cheer and compelling inferior races to bow in the dust before her'. This overcoloured and somewhat unfair picture, more true of Parkes than of Bowring, was, like similar attacks on their father's conduct in China, passed over almost in silence by Bowring's family, several of whom had their own reservations about his Chinese policy.

Not all reminiscences of the deceased Bowring were, indeed, hostile. A former editor of the *New Monthly*, whose memoirs were published in 1883 and who confessed to not sharing Bowring's political views, praised his advocacy 'of many good and useful measures in Parliament'. 'He is one whom his native county may be proud to rank among worthies of Devon'. It was not until some years after G. Barnett Smith's *Dictionary of National Biography* article on Bowring, from which anything that was unpalatable was omitted, that the main furore over Bowring's career took place. This was the publication in 1889, nearly 30 years after Bowring's death and 20 years after Borrow's death, by an American scholar, William Knapp, of *The Life, Writings and Correspondence of George Borrow*. In this biography Knapp, who had obtained no assistance from Bowring's family, fully endorsed Borrow's version of Bowring's conduct. 'It seemed to be Borrow's destiny', he declared, 'to add one more to the number of "friendless young men" who were unconsciously labouring to lift their principal on the tramway that led to government employment, to Parliament and then to the fast train to Hong Kong'. Knapp's indictment gave great offence to the surviving members of Bowring's family such as Frederick, to whom, according to Knapp, Borrow had once sneered 'Oh! Fellows of Trinity always marry their bedmakers'.

Efforts were made to counteract the influence of Knapp's book. In 1908 R. A. J. Walling published his *George Borrow – The Man and His Work*. Walling had been allowed to see the part of Bowring's correspondence relating to Borrow. He went to considerable pains to reverse the impression given by Knapp that Bowring, 'a considerable philologist', had been 'a literary pirate and a morally reprehensible cheat ... trading for cheap glory on other people's lack of knowledge'. 'It seems almost necessary', he added, 'to apologise even at this distance of time to the descendants of Sir John Bowring, so virulent and unjust is Borrow in his strictures'. The defence of Bowring carried out by Walling was taken further by several other biographers who now in rapid succession published their lives of Borrow. According to Edward Thomas, whose *George Borrow – the Man and His Books* appeared in 1912, Walling had 'brushed off the mud' thrown at Bowring by Borrow and Knapp, 'in a satisfactory manner'. By this date few of Bowring's immediate family were still alive. John had died in 1893, Maria in 1899, Lewin and Edgar in 1910 and 1911. But Frederick, though long retired from the law, was still active and assisted Herbert Jenkins in preparing yet another life of Borrow in which it was conceded that Borrow had made every possible use of Bowring's services and that Bowring 'was a man who had no hesitation in seizing everything that presented itself and turning it, as far as possible, to his own uses'. In 1913 Clement King Shorter, who had obtained the assistance of one of Bowring's grandsons, paid tribute in *George Borrow and his Circle* to Bowring's 'extraordinary energies'

No. LXXX.—MR. L. B. BOWRING, C.S.I.

THE BOWRINGS are an old Devonshire family; they formerly held Bowringsleigh, near Kingsbridge, and afterwards settled at Chulmleigh. One of the earliest mentioned in Burke's "Landed Gentry" is John Bowring who in 1680 was given leave under the Toleration Act to hold religious service in his house at Chulmleigh, Devon. His son, also John Bowring, born 1680, was a poet. But the most distinguished member of this family was Sir John Bowring,

Knight, of Claremont, Devon, LL.D., F.R.S., J.P., and D.L. He was returned as member of Parliament for Kilmarnock, N.B., in 1835, and for Bolton in 1841. He was Governor, Commander-in-Chief, and Vice-Admiral of Hongkong, and H.M. Plenipotentiary in China, Grand Cross of the Order of Leopold, and Envoy Extraordinary to Siam, and knighted at Buckingham Palace, February 16th, 1854. Sir John was born in 1792, and died 1872. He was a remarkable linguist, and a literary man of great eminence, to which his numerous works and translations attest.

Mr. Lewis Bentham Bowring, the subject of this sketch, was born at Hackney in the year 1824, his mother being the daughter of Samuel Lewin, of Hackney. He received his education at Mount Radford School, Exeter, and afterwards at the E.I. College, Haileybury, where he won prizes; also two prize medals and a Degree of Honour at Fort William College, Calcutta. From 1843 to 1870 he served in the Indian Civil Service. He was Assistant-Resident at Lahore in 1847, and private secretary to Earl Canning, when Governor-General of India from 1858 to 1862. He was Chief Commissioner of Mysore and Coorg, 1862 to 1870, and received the decoration of C.S.I. (Companion of the Star of India) in 1867. He gave up public life in 1870, and settled down at Torquay, where, with the exception of a few years in London, he has resided ever since. He is the senior county magistrate for the Torquay Division of Devon, and was for three years an alderman of the Devon County Council. He has also been Justice of the Peace for his native county since 1872.

Mr. Bowring was for five years a member of the old Local Board of Torquay, the governing body which preceded the Town Council upon the Incorporation of the town as a municipal borough. Of this obsolete body he was for three years chairman, and did good service to the town. Like his father and his brothers, Mr. Bowring has tastes of a literary and scientific character. He is also, like Sir John Bowring, an accomplished .... whenever the interesting and valuable

Lewin Bentham Bowring, 1904 Newspaper cutting in West Country Studies Library, Exeter

adding that 'in addition to being the possessor of great learning, he was a man of high character'.

Time, however, was moving on and fresh information about Bowring's literary activities was coming to light. The publication of his correspondence with continental scholars was providing evidence somewhat more in favour of Borrow's and Knapp's interpretation of events. Conversely, the publication of documents dealing with British diplomacy in China was revealing that Bowring's 'gunboat diplomacy' had been adopted by his predecessors and was carried on by his successors. (Elgin's destruction of the Imperial Summer Palace at Peking in 1860 now seemed a more cold-blooded action than Bowring's attack on Canton.) It is doubtful, however, if many of Bowring's descendants were aware of the implications of the fresh evidence. Frederick died in 1917 during the First World War at the age of 94, 'full of rich anecdotes about his undergraduate days and warmly attached to Trinity'. In 1920, when Edith who, like Maria and Frederick, never married, passed away at the age of 89, the ill-feeling about the controversial aspects of Bowring's life was beginning to diminish. The sale of his correspondence by his descendants after the Second World War and the purchase of much of it by publicly accessible institutions, such as The John Rylands Library in Manchester, at last made it possible for researchers to take a more dispassionate view of Bowring's astonishingly varied career. His offspring included a Hong Kong merchant, a barrister-at-law, a colonial administrator, a civil servant turned MP and a Jesuit priest: also two cultivated maiden ladies and a Catholic nun. But none of them achieved the eminence or provoked the controversy of their larger-than-life, 'Old Radical' father.

Main Sources and Further Reading

1. The Old Radical when Young

For Bowring's early years the main source remains *The Autobiographical Recollections of Sir John Bowring*, edited by his son L. B. Bowring (1876). This can be supplemented by the memoir in Lady D. Bowring's *A Memorial Volume of Sacred Poetry* (1873). A recent study of *The Bowring ancestry* by Joyce Youings (including a contemporary map of the Larkbear area) forms one of the collection of papers delivered at a conference held in Exeter in October 1992 and published under the title *Sir John Bowring, 1792–1872: Aspects of his Life and Career*, ed. J. Youings (Exeter 1993) (hereafter *Aspects*). For the Lewin family and Bowring's early married life, see 'The diaries of T. Asline Ward' in *Peeps into the Past*, ed. A. B. Bell (1909). Bowring's imprisonment at Boulogne is described in his *Details of the Arrest, Imprisonment and Liberation of an Englishman* (1823), but is more revealingly covered in the Carpenter MSS held at Manchester College, Oxford.

The Bentham papers in the British Library (especially Additional MSS 33545 and 35563) and at University College, London (especially boxes X, XII, XIII and CLXXIII) cover Bowring's association with Bentham and Chadwick and the dispute over Bentham's will. For the *Westminster Review* see G. L. Nesbitt, *Benthamite Reviewing: The first twelve years of the Westminster Review, 1824–1836* (New York, 1934), Bowring's memoir of Bentham is in vols. X and XI of *The Collected Works of Jeremy Bentham*, ed. J. Bowring (1843). See also G. F. Bartle, 'Jeremy Bentham and John Bowring: A study of the relationship between Bentham and the editor of his Collected Works', *Bulletin of Institute of Historical Research*, XXXVI, No. 93 (1963) and F. Rosen, 'John Bowring and the world of Jeremy Bentham', *Aspects* (1993). For Bowring and Spain, see R. Hitchcock, 'John Bowring, Hispanist and translator of Spanish poetry', *Aspects* (1993).

2. The Young Radical in Trouble

For Bowring and Greece, *Les Philhellènes et la guerre de l'indépendance* ed. E. Dalleggio (Athens, 1949) contains the correspondence of the Greek deputies Orlandos and Louriottes in London. See also D. Dakin, *British and American Philhellenes during the Greek War of Independence, 1821–1833* (Thessalonika, 1955) and F. Rosen, *Bentham, Byron and Greece: Constitutionalism, Nationalism and Early Liberal Political Thought* (Oxford, 1992). For the Greek loan scandals see G. F. Bartle, 'Bowring and the Greek loans of 1824 and 1825' in *Balkan Studies*, III (1962). The *Times* revelations about the Greek loans were printed in the October and November issues for 1826; Cobbett's attack is in *Cobbett's Political Register* LX (1826).

Two contemporary diaries mentioning Bowring in his earlier years are the diary of Henry Crabb Robinson, vol. VIII (Dr Williams's Library, London) and the diary of Francis Place (especially British Library Additional MSS 35146). Published diaries and memoirs include J. Neal, *Wandering Recollections of a Somewhat Busy Life* (Boston, Mass., 1869); C. MacFarlane, *Reminiscences of a Literary Life* (1917); E. Fox, *Memoirs of Eliza Fox* (1869). Bowring's relations with his foreign verse collaborators were described in several articles published in Europe and the USA, notably in R. Beer, *Korrespondence Johna Bowringa da Čech*, (Prague, 1904). An appendix entitled 'Bowring's verse translations' is attached to my MA thesis, 'The Political Career of Sir John Bowring between 1820 and 1849', University of London, 1959 (hereafter 'Thesis'). For Bowring's Unitarian beliefs and activities, see R. K. Webb, 'John Bowring and Unitarianism', *Utilitas*, IV, No. 1 (1992). For Bowring's business disasters, see Broughton (Hobhouse) Papers, British Library Additional MSS 36464 (especially fo. 64). The 1828 letter from Colonel Groves Jones to Revd R. Aspland and Bowring's letter of 1826 about his *Matins and Vespers* are both in my possession. The childhood letters from Frederick Bowring to his parents and from Bowring to his wife are in the Bowring collection at the John Rylands University Library, Manchester (English MSS. 1230 and 1231).

3. The Radical Doctor

For Bowring's commercial missions on the continent and in the Near East between 1830 and 1839, see the Clarendon Papers in the Bodleian Library, Oxford (Files 466, 525, 544 and 546). These include Bowring's letters to Poulett Thomson as well as to George Villiers. Other collections of Bowring's correspondence about his commercial missions are in the Granville Papers (Public Record Office (PRO) 30/29/16), the Auckland Papers (British Library Additional MSS 34459) and Foreign Office Papers (PRO F.O. 78/323, F.O. 78/345 and F.O. 97/326). These include Bowring's letters from Egypt and Prussia to Palmerston. For Bowring's Egyptian correspondence, see also the Hekekyan Papers (British Library Additional MSS 37461). Bowring's reports on his various financial and commercial missions (held at the State Paper Room in the British Library) are listed in G. F. Bartle, Summary of Theses, *Bulletin of Institute of Historical Research*, XXXIII, No. 88 (1960); (see also 'Thesis' itself). For Bowring's financial and commercial missions and his relations with political leaders see G. F. Bartle, 'Bowring and the Near Eastern crisis of 1838–1840', *English Historical Review*, LXXIX, No. 313 (1964); S. Conway, 'Bowring in government service', *Aspects* (1993); S. Conway, 'Bowring and the nineteenth century peace movement', *Historical Research*, LXIV, (1991); and R. H. Parker, 'Bowring and financial reform: accountancy and decimalisation', *Aspects* (1993). See also G. Villiers, *A Vanished Victorian: Being the Life of George Villiers, Fourth Earl of Clarendon* (1938). Carlyle's description of Bowring is in *Thomas Carlyle: Letters to his Wife* ed. T. Bliss (1953). The Bowring family correspondence is in Rylands, Eng. MSS 1229, 1230 and 1231. Invaluable for Bowring's family affairs is S. S. Hennell, *A Memoir of Charles Christian Hennell* (1899). For Bowring's attempts to get into Parliament, see Caroline Fox, *Memoirs of Old Friends*, 2 vols. (1882), as well as anecdotes in Bowring's *Autobiographical Recollections*. See also files of the *Blackburn Gazette* and *Blackburn Alfred* (1832). See A. Prentice, *The Anti-Corn Law League* (1853) for Bowring's free trade activities. Useful as a source, as well as in its own right, is J. Bowring, *Minor Morals for Young People*, 3 vols. (London and Edinburgh, 1834–39).

4. The Member of Parliament for Bolton

Bowring's speeches in the House of Commons are reported in *Hansard's Parliamentary Debates*, 3rd series, vols. XXVI-XXVIII (1835–37) and vols. LIX-CXIX (1841–48). Descriptions of him as MP are given in *Illustrated London News* (December 1842) and *Pictorial Times* (June 1844). See also G. H. Francis, *Orators of the Age* (1847) and an unidentified newspaper cutting in Rylands, Eng. MSS 351. His part in the campaign for decimal coinage is described in G. F. Bartle, 'The Decimal Coinage Agitation in the nineteenth century' in *Contemporary Review*, January 1963, and also in Parker (listed above). For the Peoples International League, consult W. J. Linton, *Memories* (1895). Two of Bowring's speeches from which extracts are quoted are *The Political and Commercial Importance of Peace* (1846) and *The Press and the People: A Report of the Proceedings connected with the Opening of the Barker Steam Press* (1846). For Bowring's business interests in Wales, see *The Cambrian* (1843–45) and *Parliamentary Papers* (1846), XXIV (Llynvi Iron Company); for his interests in railways, *Herapath's Railway and Commercial Journal* (1845–47). A detailed list of Bowring's railway shares is given in 'Thesis', quoting *Railway Subscription Contracts, Parliamentary*

Papers (1845) XL and XLVII. See also D. M. Evans, *The City or the Physiology of London Business* (1845 edn.). The letters of 1846 from Bowring to Ellice and Ellice to Russell are in the Russell Papers (PRO 30/22/5). Bowring's family correspondence is in Rylands, Eng. MSS 1229, 1230 and 1231. *Hennell* is again important for family matters. My assessment of Bowring's political career between 1820 and 1849 is in *Bulletin of Institute of Historical Research*, XXXIII, No. 88 (1960).

5. Her Britannic Majesty's Consul at Canton
The family correspondence is in Rylands, Eng. MSS 1228 (Letters to Edgar Bowring), 1229 (Correspondence with Frederick Bowring), 1230 (Bowring's miscellaneous correspondence and papers), 1231 (Frederick Bowring's correspondence), 1232 (Frederick Bowring's diary). Bowring's correspondence with Lord Clarendon is in the Clarendon Deposit. C 8 (Bodleian Library, Oxford). M. Collis, *Foreign Mud*, (1946), contains contemporary maps and prints of Canton and the Pearl River estuary. For Nathaniel Hawthorne's description of Bowring, see N. Hawthorne, *Passages from the English Notebooks* 2 vols. (Boston, Mass., 1870).

6. Sir John in Trouble
Rylands Eng. MSS 1228, 1229, 1231 and 1234 (Edgar Bowring's correspondence) are, again, essential for Bowring's family affairs. For Chinese affairs, in addition to the above sources, consult the Clarendon Deposit, C 525. See also G. F. Bartle, 'Sir John Bowring and the Arrow War in China', *Bulletin of The John Rylands Library*, XLIII, No. 2 (1961) and G. F. Bartle, 'Sir John Bowring and the Chinese and Siamese commercial treaties', *Bulletin of The John Rylands Library*, XLIV, No. 2 (1962). A contemporary defence of Bowring's policy at Canton is made in 'Lammer Moor', *Bowring, Cobden and China* (1857). Lord Elgin's relations with Bowring are described in D. Hurd, *The Arrow War* (1967). See also D. Hurd, 'Sir John Bowring of Hong Kong' *History Today*, XVII (1967). S. Lane-Poole, *Life of Sir Harry Parkes*, 2 vols. (1894) is still useful. Bowring's *The Kingdom and People of Siam*, 2 vols. (1857) was republished by OUP in 1969. For Bowring as governor of Hong Kong, see G. B. Endacott, *History of Hong Kong* (1958) and G. B. Endacott, *A Biographical Sketch Book of Early Hong Kong* (Singapore, 1962). For Bowring's relations with Borrow (in addition to various older lives of Borrow), see G. F. Bartle, 'George Borrow's "Old Radical" ', *Notes and Queries*, N. S. vol. X, no. 7 (1963) and A. Frazer, 'Two men of many tongues: George Borrow and John Bowring', *Aspects* (1993).

7. The Old Radical when Old
Bowring's activities in retirement at Exeter are discussed in two papers in

Aspects: M. Laver, 'Sir John Bowring and the Devonshire dialects', and J. Stanyer, 'Struggle with the intractable: Sir John Bowring and the reform of Devon Quarter Sessions'. For Exeter affairs, see also R. S. Lambert, *The Cobbett of the West: A Study of Thomas Latimer and the Struggle between the Pulpit and the Press in Exeter* (1939). The *Transactions of the Devonshire Association* contain several papers by and about Bowring and the files of the *Western Times* cover the local election campaigns. The important letter of 1860 from Frederick to Lewin Bowring is in Rylands, Eng. MSS 1231, the letter of 1861 from Bowring to Russell is in PRO 30/22/73 and Bowring's letter of 1871 to Gladstone in British Library Additional MSS 44431/235. Bowring's letter of 1866 to Mary Carpenter is in my possession. Official documents accrediting Bowring to the governments of Siam and the Hawaian Islands are in Rylands, Eng. MSS 1230. Bowring's decorations are listed in *Foreign Office List* (1873). Amongst many obituaries of Bowring, note *Western Times* (quoting *Daily Telegraph*), 26 November 1872. For posthumous attacks on Bowring's literary reputation, see especially W. I. Knapp, *Life of George Borrow* 2 vols. (1899). For praise of Bowring's useful measures in Parliament, see S. C. Hall, *Retrospect of a Long Life* (1883).

Index

136

Villiers George Earl of Clarendon
9, 13, 35, 40–42, 44, 49, 55,
56, 62, 66, 86–88, 97–99, 105,
121
Victoria Queen 48, 88

Walmsley Sir Joshua 67
Ward Anne 5, 7, 18

Ward Thomas Asline 5, 6, 27, 51, 77,
106
Wellington Duke of 4, 29
Western Times 111, 121
Westminster Review 18, 23, 25, 29,
30, 40, 58, 63
Wordsworth William 9

Yeh Ming-Chen 9, 89, 96, 97, 103